LEISURE ARTS PRESENTS

# GREAT AMERICAN QUILTS

BOOK FOUR

*Compiled and Edited by*

Carol L. Newbill

Oxmoor House®

©1996 by Oxmoor House, Inc.
Book Division of Southern Progress Corporation
P.O. Box 2463, Birmingham, AL 35201

Published by Oxmoor House, Inc., and Leisure Arts, Inc.

Library of Congress Catalog Card Number: 86-62283
ISBN: 0-8487-1526-8
ISSN: 1076-7673
Manufactured in the United States of America
Second Printing 2002

Editor-in-Chief: Nancy Fitzpatrick Wyatt
Senior Crafts Editor: Susan Ramey Cleveland
Senior Editor, Editorial Services: Olivia Kindig Wells
Art Director: James Boone

## Great American Quilts Book Four

Editor: Carol Logan Newbill
Editorial Assistant: Cecile Y. Nierodzinski
Copy Editor: Susan S. Cheatham
Production and Distribution Director: Phillip Lee
Associate Production Managers: Theresa L. Beste,
    Vanessa D. Cobbs
Production Coordinator: Marianne Jordan Wilson
Production Assistant: Valerie Heard
Designer: Teresa Kent
Patterns and Illustrations: Kelly Davis
Publishing Systems Administrator: Rick Tucker
Senior Photographer: John O'Hagan
Photo Stylist: Katie Stoddard

# EDITOR'S NOTE

Quilters have a long-standing love affair with the natural world. Sunflowers, irises, maple leaves, flying geese, and stars of all kinds grace countless quilts, both new and old. For this year's special chapter, we have chosen six wonderful quilts reflecting the theme of "Sea and Sky." From Joanne Barton's elegantly simple *Ocean Wave* to Meg Simle's exuberant *Happy Fish*, these quilts use color, pattern, and rhythm to celebrate the world through fabric.

Bobbi Finley's *Wasatch Memories* brings a splash of autumn color to "Quilts Across America." And fans of Christmas quilts will enjoy making a sleighful of Santas like those in Jo Barry's *Santa's Helpers*.

Appliqué lovers will find plenty to please them in "Traditions in Quilting," including Eula Long's *Basket Quilt*, an original design of 12 baskets filled with flowers, fruit, and birds. Both Beth Anderson and Cindy Hamilton—one in Texas, the other in Colorado—based their very different quilts on photographs of antique quilts they found in the same book! To round out our collection of 24 quilts, be sure to admire the artistry showcased in "Designer Gallery," ranging from Linda Schmidt's haunting *The Dawn of Time* to Corinne Appleton's tongue-in-cheek *A Tail of 12 Kitties*. Enjoy!

Where do our Great American quilters come from? They come from Florida and Oregon, from Idaho and Georgia, from New Mexico and New York. This year's book features quilts from quilters and quilting groups in 15 different states across America.

If your state isn't represented, let us put a star on next year's map for you! For information on submitting a quilt, write to *Great American Quilts* Editor, Oxmoor House, 2100 Lakeshore Drive, Birmingham, AL 35209.

# Sea & Sky

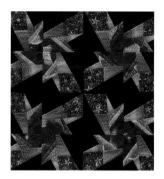

# Quilts Across America

# Traditions in Quilting

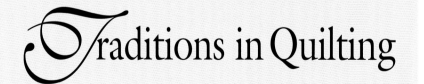

# E N T S

## Bee Quilters

## Designer Gallery

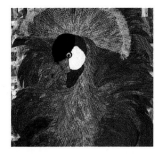

## Quilt Smart Workshop

# Sea & Sky

## Helen White
### Ukiah, California

"*I* grew up in Norway," says Helen White. "I came to this country to go to school, intending to stay for one year and return home. Then I met this nice guy, and the rest is history!"

Although she had learned knitting and embroidery as a child, Helen lived in the United States for 15 years before she discovered quilts. "I went into a fabric store looking for elastic to mend my son's pajamas," she says. "Behind the counter was a beautiful wall hanging advertising a quilting class, and I fell in love with quilts then and there. I didn't buy the elastic, but I signed up for my first quilt class!"

*"I'm always looking for shortcuts. They get me to the next quilt faster!"*

Since then, Helen has taken a number of classes from nationally known teachers, including Michael James and Doreen Speckmann, and she finds time each day for quilting. "I'm still at the learning stage, trying out this and that," she says. "Quilting appeared in my life at a very opportune time."

## Night Sky
### 1995

"I love stars," Helen says. "I wanted to make a big star quilt, so I chose this project for the week-long retreat at Point Bonita in January of 1995." Because Doreen Speckmann is one of the artists in residence at Point Bonita each year, Helen chose to adapt a quilt shown in Doreen's book *Pattern Play*. (See "Resources," page 144.) The star block uses the long- and short-legged unit Doreen calls "Mutt and Jeff." Helen changed the layout of Doreen's star blocks, modified them for paper piecing, and added a checkerboard border of her own design. "Paper piecing is a useful technique, especially if the pieces have lots of stretchy bias edges," Helen says. "It's often a shortcut, and I'm always looking for shortcuts. They get me to the next quilt faster!"

# Night Sky

## Finished Quilt Size
78" x 90"

## Fabric Requirements
| | |
|---|---|
| Blue prints | 5¾ yards |
| Yellow prints | 3 yards |
| Brown prints | ½ yard |
| Backing | 5½ yards |
| Dark blue for binding | ¾ yard |

## Pieces to Cut
Assorted blue prints
  136 A
  162 E
  828 F
  4 G
  4 H
Assorted yellow prints
  272 B
  136 C
  820 F
Assorted brown prints
  34 D

## Quilt Top Assembly
**1.** Referring to photograph for color placement and to *Block 1 Assembly Diagram*, join 1 A, 1 B, and 1 C as shown to make 1 Block 1. Repeat to make 136 Block 1s.

*Block 1 Assembly Diagram Make 136.*

**2.** Referring to photograph for color placement and to *Block 2 Assembly Diagram*, join 4 Bs and 1 D as shown to make 1 Block 2. Repeat to make 34 Block 2s.

*Block 2 Assembly Diagram Make 34.*

**3.** In same manner, join 7 yellow Fs and 9 blue Fs as shown in *Block 3 Assembly Diagram* to make 1 Block 3. Repeat to make 2 Block 3s.

*Block 3 Assembly Diagram Make 2.*

**4.** Referring to *Block 4 Assembly Diagram*, join 6 yellow Fs and 10 blue Fs to make 1 block 4. Repeat to make 2 Block 4s.

*Block 4 Assembly Diagram Make 2.*

**5.** Join 1 yellow F, 1 G, and 1 H as shown in *Block 5 Assembly Diagram* to make 1 Block 5. Repeat to make 4 Block 5s.

*Block 5 Assembly Diagram
Make 4.*

**6.** Referring to *Quilt Top Assembly Diagram* and to photograph for color placement, join blocks and blue Es in 20 rows of 17 blocks each, rotating Blocks 3, 4, and 5 as shown. Join rows.

**7.** To make 1 side pieced border, join 40 yellow Fs and 40 blue Fs alternately to make 1 row. Repeat to make 5 rows. Join rows, alternating colors in checkerboard fashion as shown in photograph. Repeat to make second side pieced border. Join to sides of quilt.

**8.** To make top pieced border, join 39 yellow Fs and 39 blue Fs alternately to make 1 row. Repeat to make 5 rows. Join rows, alternating colors. Join to top of quilt. Repeat to make and join bottom pieced border.

## Quilting
Quilt around all pieces, ¼" inside seam lines, or quilt as desired.

## Finished Edges
Bind with bias binding made from dark blue.

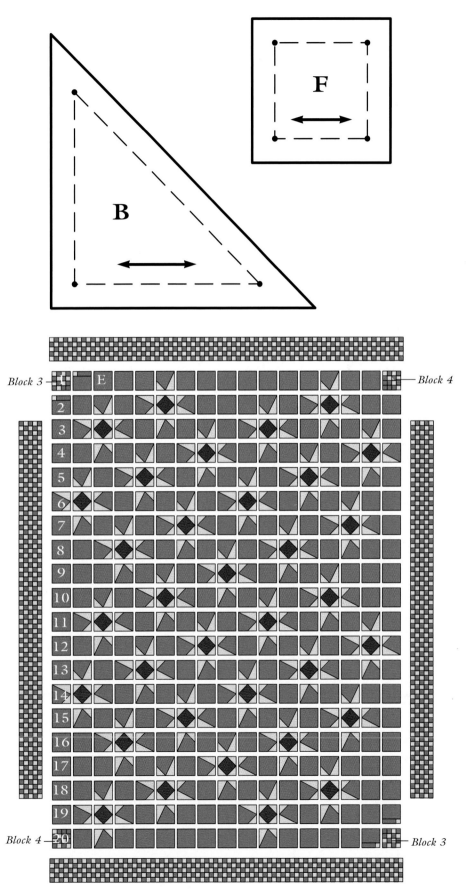

*Quilt Top Assembly Diagram*

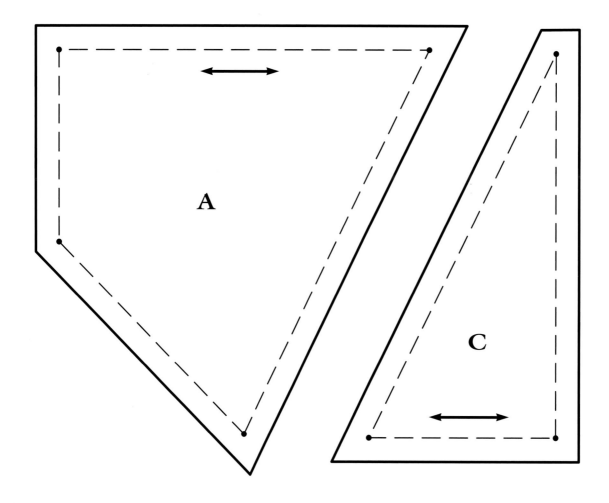

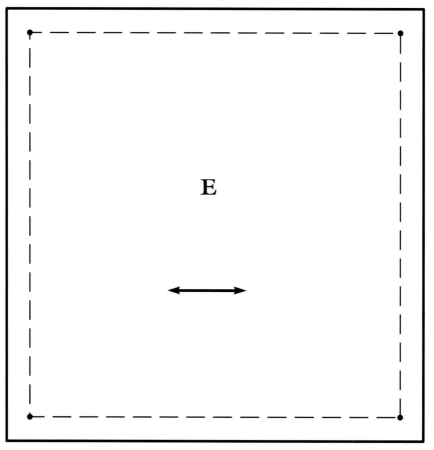

A

C

E

12

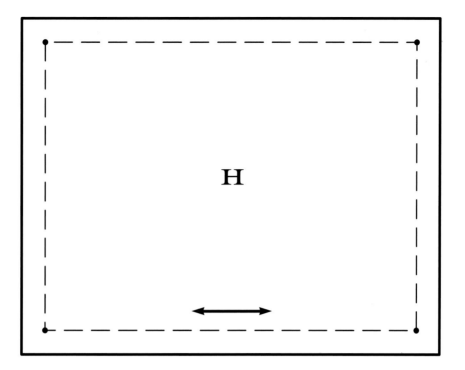

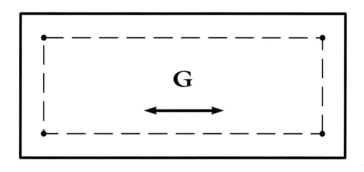

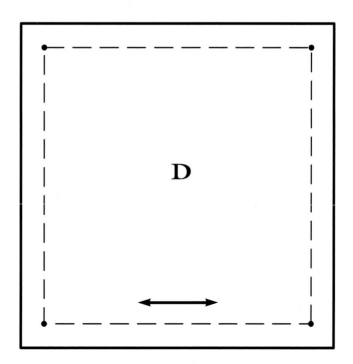

# Joanna Lotts
Natural Bridge, Virginia

"*I*'ve always enjoyed things you do with your hands," says Joanna Lotts. "Sewing, knitting, or cross-stitch—anything with yarn or thread or fabric." With a college major in clothing and textiles, and a large collection of scraps from sewing for three children, Joanna's progression into quiltmaking was natural. She began by making wall hangings and baby quilts, portable projects that she could take to the doctor's office or the ball park while waiting for her children. With several women of her church, Joanna organized a group that makes quilts for area nursing and children's homes. They also make a raffle quilt each year as a fund-raising project for the local civic group.

*"I have dreams and fabric for more quilts than I will ever make."*

Joanna isn't planning to slow down any time soon. "Once my children are out of high school," she says, "I'd like to start teaching quilting in the community. It's a great way to meet new friends."

## Mama's Quilt
1995

During the winter of 1993–94, Joanna's mother moved from the house she had lived in for 35 years. To her sorrow, she found that the cardinals that had always come to her bird feeder in her old house did not find their way to the new one. "I made this quilt so that Mama would have cardinals," Joanna says. "I planned it as a wall hanging, but it just seemed to grow!"

For the central blocks, Joanna enlarged the cardinal blocks shown in Margaret Rolfe's *Go Wild With Quilts*. (See "Resources," page 144.) For the borders, she decided to use some blocks that she had made for another piece but never used. "After I started sewing it together," she says, "I found that the pieced borders were a little short. So I added a small strip to the corner so

everything would fit. That's one of the fun things about quilting—just add a little bit here and there."

The new house had a perfect place to hang *Mama's Quilt*, on a wall above the stairway to the second floor where Joanna's mother could see her cardinals every day. And the following winter, a pair of cardinals found their way to the new feeder in the back yard.

## Mama's Quilt

### Finished Quilt Size
75" x 75"

### Fabric Requirements

| | |
|---|---|
| White | 3 yards |
| Black | 2¼ yards |
| Red print 1 | ⅛ yard |
| Red print 2 | ⅛ yard |
| Red print 3 | 1 yard |
| Blue floral | ⅝ yard |
| Light blue/<br>pink floral | ¼ yard |
| Dark blue/<br>purple floral | 1 yard |
| White floral | ¼ yard |
| Green floral | 2¼ yards |
| Backing | 4¾ yards |
| Black for binding | ¾ yard |

### Pieces to Cut

White
  4 (6½" x 56¼") borders
  4 (6½" x 20") borders
  8 (6½") border squares
  2 (9⅞") squares for A*

  4 C
  4 E
  4 L
  1 (7⅞") square for Ms*
  4 N
  32 Y
  32 Y rev.
  4 AA

Black
  2 (1¼" x 75¼") borders
  2 (1¼" x 73¾") borders
  2 (1¼" x 69¼") borders
  2 (1¼" x 68¼") borders
  2 (1" x 42¾") borders
  2 (1" x 41¾") borders
  2 (1" x 33") borders
  2 (1" x 32") borders
  4 I

Red print 1
  4 B
  4 G
  4 H
  4 J
  4 K

Red print 2
  4 D
  4 F

Red print 3
  56 O
  4 R
  56 (1⅝"–square) V**
  4 BB
  4 CC

Blue floral
  1 (7⅞") square for Ms*
  6 (8") squares for Z*
  56 (1⅝" x 4⅛") W**
  4 BB

Light blue/pink floral
  28 (3"–square) T**

Dark blue/purple floral
  8 P
  8 P rev.
  104 Q
  16 S

White floral
  56 (1⅝" x 3") U

Green floral
  4 (2¾" x 73¾") borders
  32 X

*See Step 1.
**Rotary-cut these pieces; no pattern given.

### Quilt Top Assembly

**1.** To make 4 As, cut 9⅞" white squares in half diagonally. Referring to *Cutting Diagram for A*, remove 1 corner of each triangle as shown. To make 4 white Ms, cut 7⅞" white square into quarters diagonally. To make 4 blue Ms, cut 7⅞" blue floral square into quarters diagonally. To make 24 Zs, cut 8" blue floral squares into quarters diagonally. Set aside.

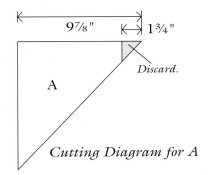

*Cutting Diagram for A*

**2.** Referring to *Cardinal Block Assembly Diagram*, join 1 each of pieces A-L, 1 white M, 1 blue floral M, and 1 N to make 1 Cardinal block. Repeat to make 4 blocks. Join blocks, rotating as shown in photograph, to make center medallion.

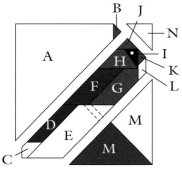

*Cardinal Block Assembly Diagram*

**3.** Join 2 (6½" x 20") white border strips to sides of center medallion as shown in *Quilt Top Assembly Diagram*.

**4.** Join 1 (6½") white square to each end of remaining 2 (6½" x 20") white border strips. Join to top and bottom of quilt, butting corners.

**5.** Join 1" x 32" black border strips to top and bottom of quilt. Join 1" x 33" black border strips to sides of quilt, butting corners.

**6.** To make 1 inner pieced border, join 14 Os, 2 Ps, 2 Ps rev., and 26 Qs as shown in *Inner Border Assembly Diagram*. Repeat to make 4 borders. Join 2 borders to sides of quilt.

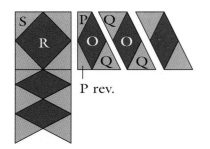

*Inner Border Assembly Diagram*

**7.** To make 1 pieced corner block, join 1 R and 4 Ss as shown. Repeat to make 4 blocks. Join 1 pieced corner block to each end of remaining inner pieced borders. Join borders to top and bottom of quilt, butting corners.

**8.** Join 1" x 41¾" black border strips to top and bottom of quilt. Join 1" x 42¾" black border strips to sides of quilt, butting corners.

**9.** Join 1 T, 2 Us, 2 Vs, and 2 Ws as shown in *Outer Border Assembly Diagram* to make 1 pieced square. Repeat to make 28 pieced squares. Join 1 X, 1 Y, and 1 Y rev. as shown to make 1 pieced triangle. Repeat to make 32 pieced triangles. Join 1 AA, 1 red print 3 BB, 1 blue floral BB, and 1 CC as

shown to make 1 pieced corner strip. Repeat to make 4 pieced corner strips.

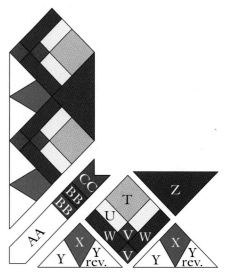

*Outer Border Assembly Diagram*

**10.** To make 1 outer pieced border, join 7 pieced squares, 8 pieced triangles, and 6 Zs as shown in *Outer Border Assembly Diagram*. Repeat to make 4

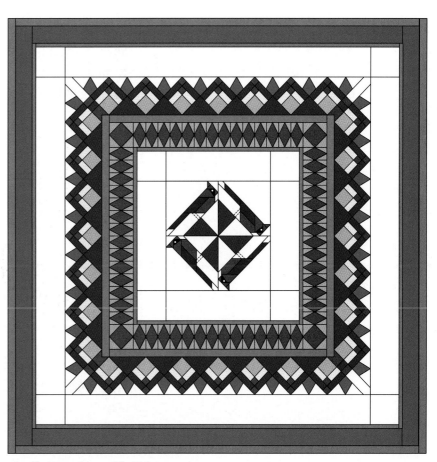

*Quilt Top Assembly Diagram*

outer pieced borders. Join 2 borders to sides of quilt.

**11.** Join 1 pieced corner strip to each end of remaining outer pieced borders. Join to top and bottom of quilt, mitering corners.

**12.** Join 2 (6½" x 56¼") white border strips to sides of quilt.

**13.** Join 1 (6½") white square to each end of remaining white border strips. Join to top and bottom of quilt, butting corners.

**14.** Join 1¼" x 68¼" black border strips to top and bottom of quilt. Join 1¼" x 69¼" black border strips to sides of quilt, butting corners.

**15.** Join 2¾" x 73¾" green floral strips to top and bottom of quilt. Join 2¾" x 73¾" green floral strips to sides of quilt, butting corners.

**16.** Join 1¼" x 73¾" black border strips to top and bottom of quilt. Join 1¼" x 75¼" black border strips to sides of quilt, butting corners.

## Quilting

Quilt around all pieces. Quilt free-form feather design in white borders as shown in photograph, or quilt as desired.

## Finished Edges

Bind with bias binding made from black.

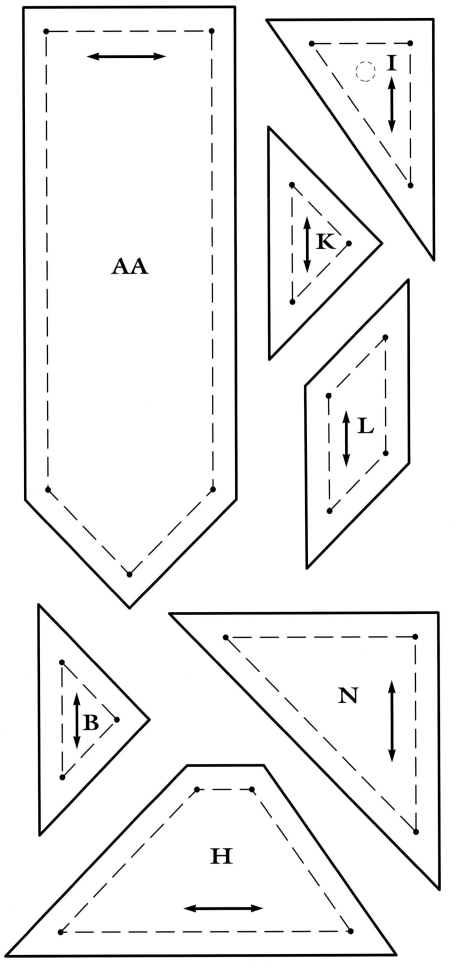

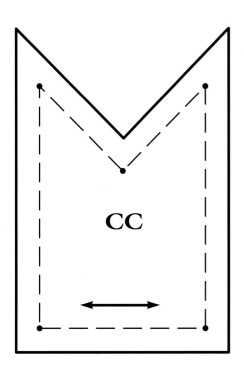

**CC**

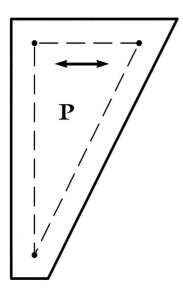

**P**

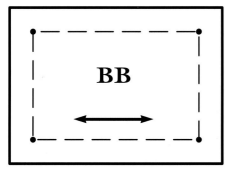

**BB**

❖ QUILT SMART ❖

**Joanna's Upside-Down Quilting**

Joanna Lotts had originally planned an appliquéd motif for the wide white borders of *Mama's Quilt*. She drew the patterns, cut out the pieces, and pinned the first set of pieces down, but the appliqué overpowered the central medallion. "I decided to do some decorative quilting instead," she says.

After outline-quilting the central medallion, Joanna marked the edges of the borders on the quilt's backing. She threaded her bobbin with Decor 6 decorative rayon thread and used invisible nylon thread on top of the machine. (For a mail-order source, see "Resources," page 144.) She placed the quilt on her sewing machine wrong side up, so that the rayon thread would appear on the quilt's front, and set her machine for a decorative stitch.

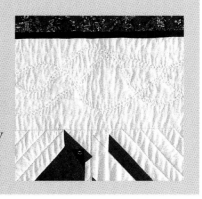

"Then I just free-motion quilted across the border area I had marked," Joanna says. "The invisible thread doesn't show on the back, but the decorative thread gives a lovely effect on the front."

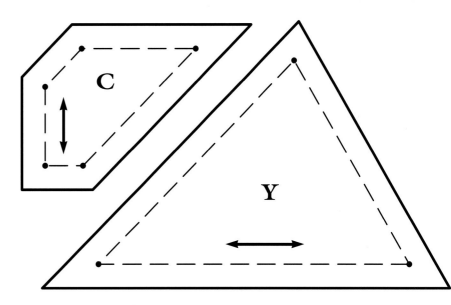

**C**

**Y**

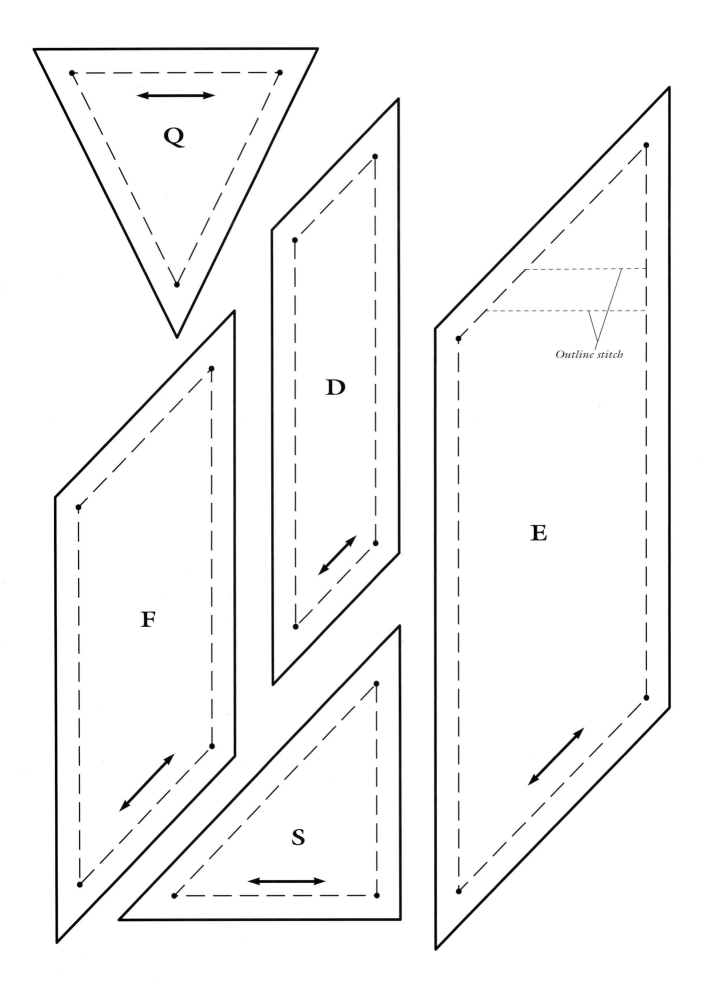

Q

D

E

Outline stitch

F

S

20

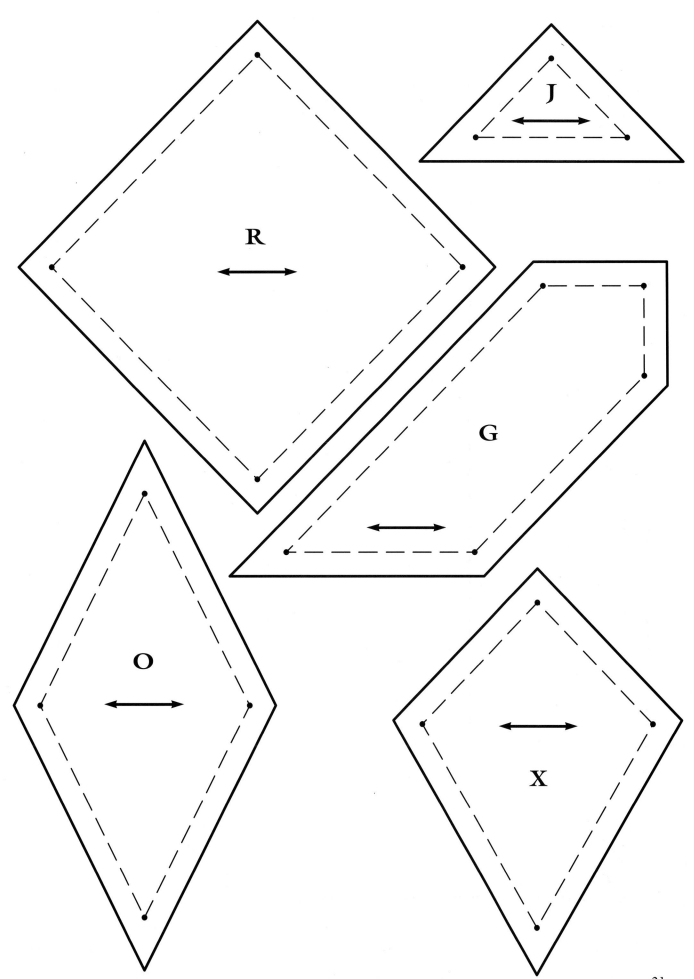

R

J

G

O

X

21

# Joanne Campen Barton
## Coos Bay, Oregon

*W*hether she is talking about color selection or planning a gift for a friend, Joanne Barton's enthusiasm for quilting bubbles joyfully through everything she says.

"How exciting to create a treasure for a special person!" she says. "The quest for the feeling or mood of the quilt, including favorite colors and interests in the design. The colors: dark or light, bold or soft; the quilting designs. Where's the graph paper? The ruler? Quick, before I lose the idea!"

*"Just quilting, with a kettle of soup simmering on the stove, my gray cat beside me—what a dream."*

Joanne began quilting in order to use some of the remnants she had accumulated from years of sewing for her family. And although those leftovers are long since gone, she somehow still has lots of fabric that she needs to make into quilts. "I'll start a new project and spend every minute possible on it," she says. "I love it all—carefully making the templates, cutting out the pieces, and placing them on my planner board to confirm the full impact of the design. The touch of the fabrics while I plan and sew is such a comfort—a wonderful creative process."

# Ocean Wave
## 1989

Joanne hesitated for a number of years before deciding to make an Ocean Waves quilt. "The pattern appealed to me, but I had never sewn that many triangles before," she says. "I was concerned about getting my points to match." So instead of beginning with a queen-size quilt, as she usually does, Joanne decided to make this small version as a practice piece.

"I had the top all pieced before I saw *Let's Make Waves,* a book devoted to Ocean Waves quilts," she says. "But mine must have turned out well anyway, because it won a Judge's Choice award at the quilt show in Bandon, Oregon, in 1991."

## Quilt Top Assembly

**1.** Referring to Block Assembly Diagram and to photograph for color placement, join 7 white As, 7 blue As, 1 white B, and 1 blue B as shown to make 1 block. Repeat to make 20 blocks.

**2.** Join blocks in 5 rows of 4 blocks each, rotating blocks as shown in *Quilt Top Assembly Diagram*. Join rows.

**3.** Join 3¾" x 40½" white border strips to sides of quilt. Join remaining white border strips to top and bottom of quilt, butting corners.

**4.** Join 1½" x 47" blue border strips to sides of quilt. Join remaining blue border strips to top and bottom of quilt, butting corners.

## Quilting

Quilt in-the-ditch around all pieces. In each B, quilt *Triangle Quilting Pattern*. In white border, quilt *Border Quilting Pattern*.

## Finished Edges

Bind with bias binding made from blue.

## Ocean Wave

### Finished Quilt Size
40½" x 46½"

### Number of Blocks and Finished Size
20 blocks      8" x 8"

### Fabric Requirements
White      1½ yards
Blue      1⅝ yards
Backing      1½ yards
Blue for binding      ½ yard

### Pieces to Cut
White
   2 (3¾" x 40½") border strips
   2 (3¾" x 39") border strips
   70 (2⅞") squares*
   10 (6⅞") squares**
Blue
   2 (1½" x 47") border strips
   2 (1½" x 41") border strips
   70 (2⅞") squares*
   10 (6⅞") squares**

*Cut in half diagonally for 140 As.
**Cut in half diagonally for 20 Bs.

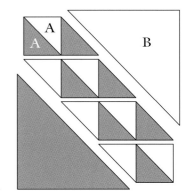

*Block Assembly Diagram*

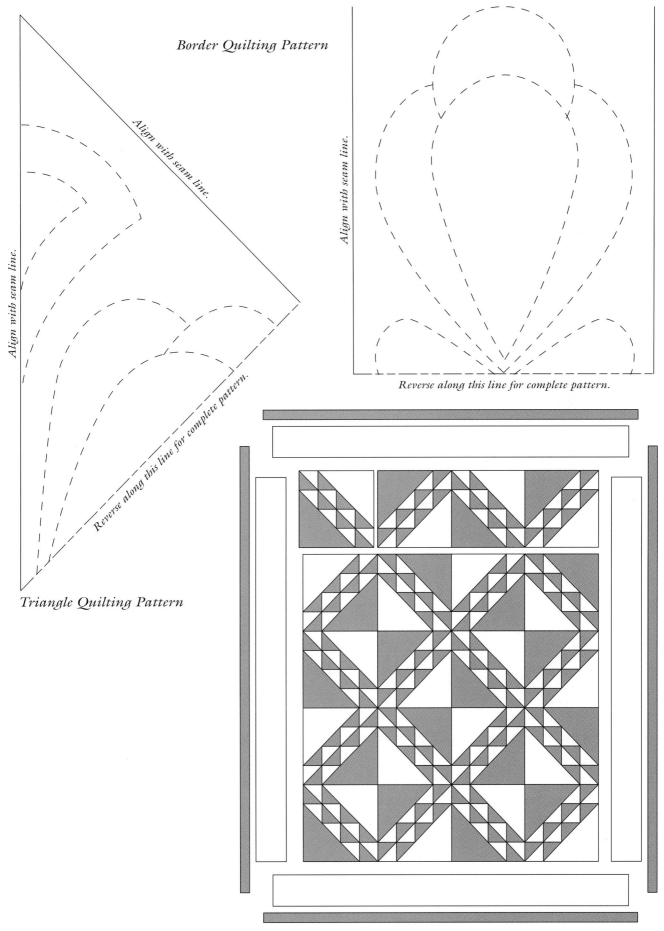

*Border Quilting Pattern*

*Align with seam line.*

*Reverse along this line for complete pattern.*

*Align with seam line.*

*Align with seam line.*

*Reverse along this line for complete pattern.*

*Triangle Quilting Pattern*

*Quilt Top Assembly Diagram*

# Jenny Frank Hubbard
Fort Collins, Colorado

"What was our living room is now the quilt room," says Jenny Hubbard. "Everyone in the family knows that it's strictly off limits!"

Fourteen years ago, Jenny found that quiltmaking offered everything she needed to express her art: color, texture, and pattern. "Quite simply, quilts are a visual pleasure," she says. Even Jenny's 1-year-old daughter gives them her stamp of approval. She loves to pull one down to the floor and lie on it!

Many of Jenny's quilts are original designs, which have been exhibited nationally as well as in shows in Japan, Italy, and France. "My quilts have traveled more extensively than I have!" Jenny says. "Until my children are older and I can satisfy my need to see the world, I'll send my quilts."

*"My quilts have traveled more extensively than I have!"*

# North by Northwest
## 1995

When she began to plan *North by Northwest,* Jenny knew she wanted a feeling of movement in the piecing as well as in the shifting colors. She played with traditional Flying Geese patches, placing them at right angles and filling in the corner, to create this block design. "I wanted the colors to migrate across the quilt," she says, "leading the viewer around the surface and inviting a closer inspection."

*North by Northwest* was one of a series of quilts Jenny made as part of a grant from the National Endowment for the Arts. It was exhibited as part of Jenny's 1995 one-artist show in Fort Collins, Colorado. It was also included in *The Artist and the Quilt,* a show of work by the Front Range Contemporary Quilters held in Denver, Colorado, in 1995.

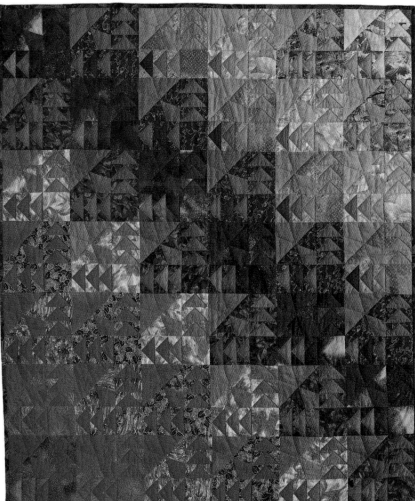

*Block design ©1994 Jenny Frank Hubbard*

## North by Northwest

### Finished Quilt Size

45" x 52½"

### Number of Blocks and Finished Size

42 blocks          7½" x 7½"

### Fabric Requirements

| | |
|---|---|
| Light green solid | scrap* |
| Light green print | scrap* |
| Medium green solid | scrap* |
| Medium green print | ⅛ yard |
| Blue-green solid | ⅛ yard |
| Blue-green print | ¼ yard |
| Light blue solid | ⅛ yard |
| Light blue print | ¼ yard |
| Medium blue solid | ⅛ yard |
| Medium blue print | ⅜ yard |
| Dark blue solid | ⅛ yard |
| Dark blue print | ½ yard |
| Blue-violet solid | ⅛ yard |
| Blue-violet print | ½ yard |
| Lavender solid | ⅛ yard |
| Lavender print | ⅜ yard |
| Red-violet solid | ⅛ yard |
| Red-violet print | ¼ yard |
| Light fuschia solid | ⅛ yard |
| Light fuschia print | ¼ yard |
| Medium fuschia solid | ⅛ yard |
| Medium fuschia print | ⅛ yard |
| Dark fuschia solid | scrap* |
| Dark fuschia print | scrap* |
| Light magenta solid | scrap* |
| Medium magenta solid | scrap* |
| Backing | 3 yards |
| Dark blue for binding | ⅝ yard |

*10" square

## Pieces to Cut

| | |
|---|---|
| **Light green solid** | **Blue-violet print** |
| 4 A | 72 B |
| 1 D | 6 C |
| 1 F | 6 E |
| **Light green print** | 6 E rev. |
| 12 B | **Lavender solid** |
| 1 C | 32 A |
| 1 E | 5 D |
| 1 E rev. | 5 F |
| **Medium green solid** | **Lavender print** |
| 9 A | 60 B |
| 2 D | 5 C |
| 2 F | 5 E |
| **Medium green print** | 5 E rev. |
| 24 B | **Red-violet solid** |
| 2 C | 27 A |
| 2 E | 4 D |
| 2 E rev. | 4 F |
| **Blue-green solid** | **Red-violet print** |
| 15 A | 48 B |
| 3 D | 4 C |
| 3 F | 4 E |
| **Blue-green print** | 4 E rev. |
| 36 B | **Light fuchsia solid** |
| 3 C | 21 A |
| 3 E | 3 D |
| 3 E rev. | 3 F |
| **Light blue solid** | **Light fuchsia print** |
| 21 A | 36 B |
| 4 D | 3 C |
| 4 F | 3 E |
| **Light blue print** | 3 E rev. |
| 48 B | **Medium fuchsia solid** |
| 4 C | 15 A |
| 4 E | 2 D |
| 4 E rev. | 2 F |
| **Medium blue solid** | **Medium fuchsia print** |
| 27 A | 24 B |
| 5 D | 2 C |
| 5 F | 2 E |
| **Medium blue print** | 2 E rev. |
| 60 B | **Dark fuchsia solid** |
| 5 C | 9 A |
| 5 E | 1 D |
| 5 E rev. | 1 F |
| **Dark blue solid** | **Dark fuchsia print** |
| 33 A | 12 B |
| 6 D | 1 C |
| 6 F | 1 E |
| **Dark blue print** | 1 E rev. |
| 72 B | **Light magenta solid** |
| 6 C | 3 A |
| 6 E | **Medium magenta solid** |
| 6 E rev. | 1 A |
| **Blue-violet solid** | |
| 35 A | |
| 6 D | |
| 6 F | |

## Quilt Top Assembly

**1.** Referring to *Block Assembly Diagram* and to photograph for color placement, join the following pieces to make 1 light-green block: 4 light green solid As, 1 medium green solid A, 1 blue-green solid A, 12 light green print Bs, 1 light green print C, 1 light green solid D, 1 light green print E, 1 light green print E rev., and 1 light green solid F.

**2.** In same manner, make 2 medium green blocks, 3 blue-green, 4 light blue, 5 medium blue, 6 dark blue, 6 blue-violet, 5 lavender, 4 red-violet, 3 light fuchsia, 2 medium fuchsia, and 1 dark fuchsia.

**3.** Referring to photograph for color arrangement, join blocks into 7 rows of 6 blocks each. Join rows.

## Quilting

Quilt in-the-ditch around all pieces. Quilt diagonal lines across each F as shown in block photograph.

## Finished Edges

Bind with bias binding made from dark blue.

*Note that each block is composed of one print fabric (12 Bs, 1 C, 1 E, 1 E rev.) and three solid fabrics (6 As, 1 D, 1 F). Four of the solid As match the D and F, while the remaining As are cut from the two next darker solids.*

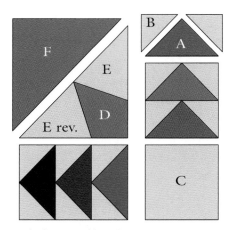

*Block Assembly Diagram*

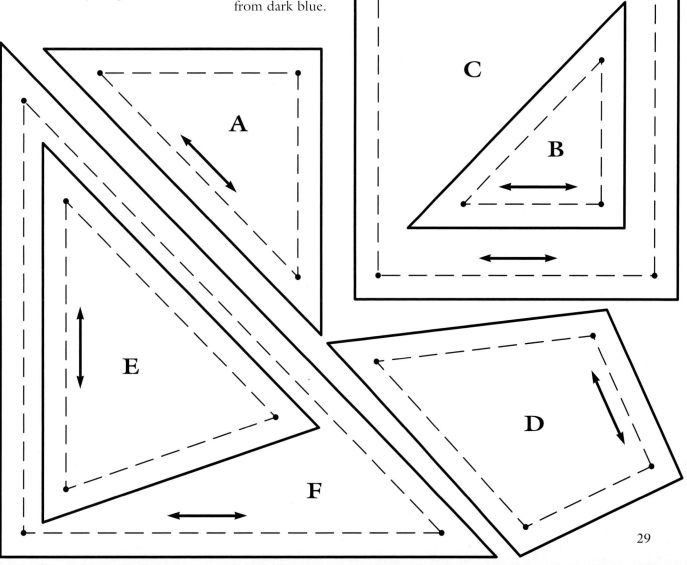

## Crane Johnson
### Eagle, Idaho

*I*t's hard to describe Crane Johnson with just a single word, although "energetic" quickly comes to mind. She loves conversation, traveling, roller blading, tai chi, fly fishing, and, of course, quilting. Her quilts sparkle with color, contrast, and the metallic thread she uses for hand quilting. "A member of the 'quilt police' told me once that it was impossible to hand-quilt with metallic thread," Crane says. "That was all it took for me to give it a try! I've been using it ever since."

*"My inspirations come from always asking 'What if?' I love making colors work dynamically."*

Crane often makes several quilts from one idea. "I love working in series," she says. "I often have more than one series going at a time."

## Apparent Magnitude
### 1995

"My son, Brian, first found the term 'apparent magnitude' in a science book," Crane says. "It's used to describe the brightness of a star as it appears from earth." Working with this idea, Crane and Brian chose star-bright colors to contrast with the night sky background. "When the quilt was finished," Crane says, "Brian convinced me that if I sent it to a show, it would win a prize." She entered the Quilters' Heritage Celebration in Lancaster, Pennsylvania. "When we got there and saw the Honorable Mention ribbon on the quilt, I don't know which of us was more excited!"

# Apparent Magnitude

## Finished Quilt Size
75¾" x 75¾"

## Number of Blocks and Finished Size
16 blocks          16" x 16"

## Fabric Requirements

| | |
|---|---|
| Black | 3 yards |
| Star print | 3¼ yards |
| Blue-green | 2¼ yards |
| Gold print | ¾ yard |
| Light blue | ½ yard |
| Orange print | 1 yard |
| Backing | 4¾ yards |
| Black for binding | ¾ yard |

## Pieces to Cut

Black
    4 (1⅛" x 77") border strips
    4 (2¼" x 77") border strips
    64 A
    64 E
Star print
    4 (2¾" x 77") border strips
    116 (3¾") squares*
    64 B
Blue-green
    4 (1¾" x 77") border strips
    64 C
    64 D
Gold print
    64 F
Light blue
    64 G
Orange print
    64 H
*For prairie points.

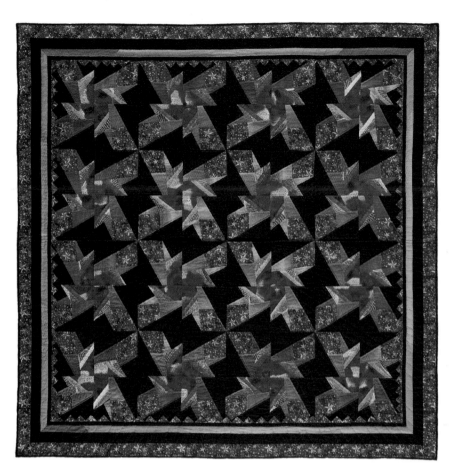

## Quilt Top Assembly

**1.** Referring to *Block Assembly Diagram*, join 1 A, 1 B, 1 C, 1 D, 1 E, 1 F, 1 G, and 1 H as shown to make 1 quarter block. Repeat to make 4 quarter blocks. Join quarters, rotating as shown, to make 1 block. Repeat to make 16 blocks.

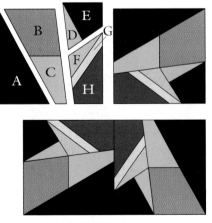

*Block Assembly Diagram*

**2.** Join blocks in 4 rows of 4 blocks each, as shown in *Quilt Top Assembly Diagram*. Join rows.

**3.** To make 1 pieced border, join border strips in the following order: 1 (1⅛" x 77") black strip, 1 (1¾" x 77") blue-green strip, 1 (2¼" x 77") black strip, and 1 (2¾" x 77") star print strip. Repeat to make 4 pieced borders. Set aside.

**4.** To make prairie point border, fold 29 star print squares into quarters as shown in *Prairie Point Diagram*. Pin prairie points to 1 edge of quilt top, aligning raw edges and overlapping points as required to fit edge of quilt. Baste. Repeat for 3 remaining edges of quilt.

**5.** With right sides facing, centers matched, and prairie points sandwiched between, join black edge of 1 pieced border to 1 edge of quilt, stitching through prairie points.

Repeat for remaining borders, mitering corners. Press prairie points toward quilt and borders outward.

*Prairie Point Diagram*

## Quilting

Quilt around all pieces, ¼" inside seam lines. Quilt diagonal lines, 1½" apart, across borders.

*Figure 1*

*Figure 2*

## Finished Edges

Bind with bias binding made from black.

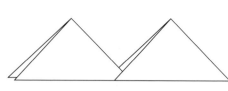

*Figure 3*

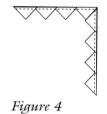

*Figure 4*

*Miter corners.*

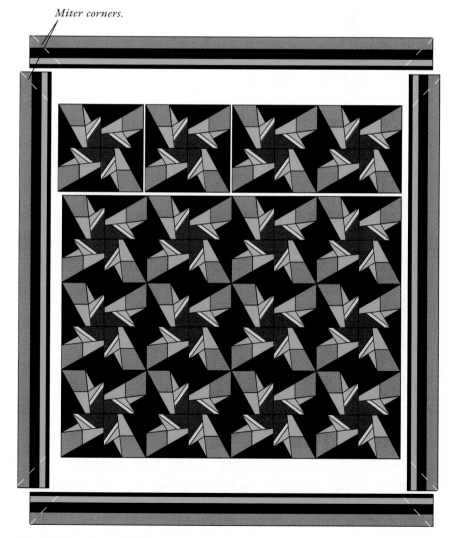

*Quilt Top Assembly Diagram*

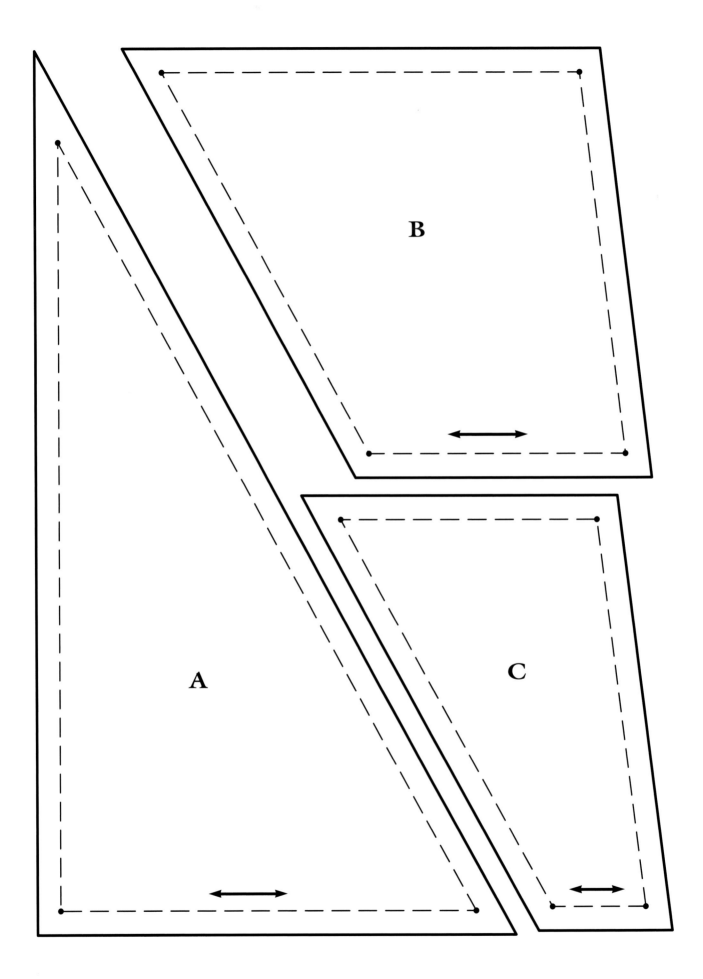

A

B

C

34

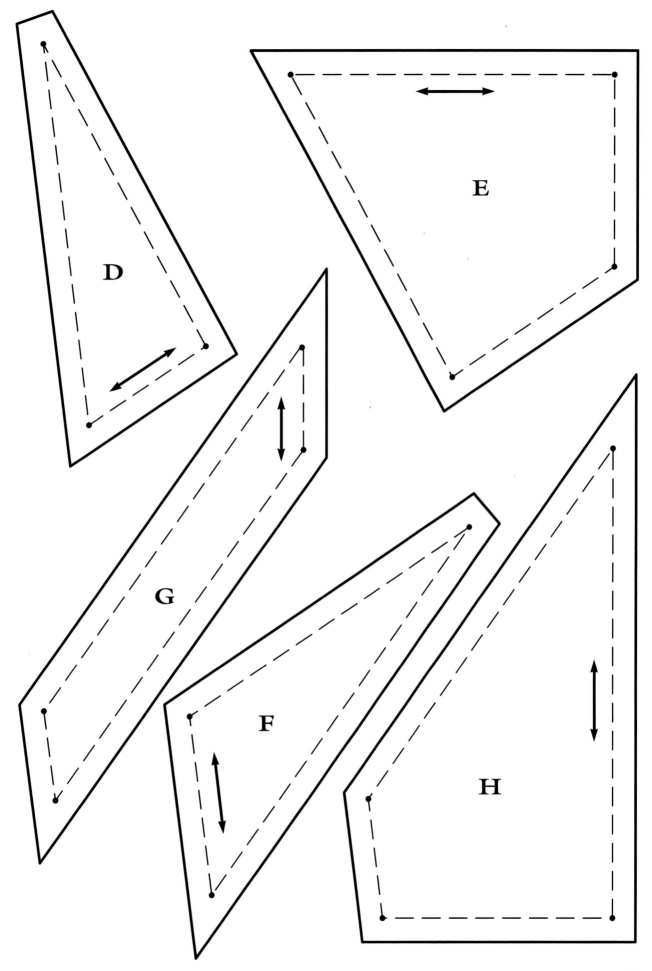

D

E

G

F

H

# Meg McKinney Simle
Birmingham, Alabama

*P*rofessional photographer Meg Simle has a job many of us would consider ideal. Covering stories for *Southern Living,* a regional magazine with a strong travel department, she takes pictures of interesting places and beautiful scenery—an endless source of ideas. She has developed an eye for color and composition that many quilters would envy. So it's no surprise to find that Meg has combined these advantages with her time on the road and her love of sewing to make quilts.

*"Quilting is a big world of creativity."*

"I sewed a lot of clothes," Meg says. "Then, when I was living in Houston, I took a class in rotary cutting and quick machine-piecing techniques, thinking I'd find new ways to do things faster. Instead, I found out that quilting was a lot more creative and much more fun."

Meg belongs to guilds both in Birmingham and in Houston, and she makes a point of finding quilt shops and quilters wherever her travels take her. "Quilting is a big world of creativity," she says. "I love meeting and working with talented, friendly people who also happen to make quilts!"

# Happy Fish
## 1995

In January of 1995, when much of the nation was buried under snowdrifts, Meg went to the Caribbean to photograph a quilting cruise featuring teacher Doreen Speckmann. But the cruise wasn't all work; Meg managed to find time to take one of Doreen's classes on "Peaky and Spike," the three-triangle unit that forms the fish's fins and tail.

"At Doreen's suggestion, I brought along my brightest and sunniest fabrics, including some I thought would *never* work together," Meg says. During the weeklong class, Doreen showed the students how to coordinate their bright mixes of unusual prints with results like those in Meg's *Happy Fish.* "It was really neat to meet quilters from all over North America, and to see that no two fabric stashes were alike," Meg says. "Yet under Doreen's direction, we all came out with sunny memories of a lovely quilting experience."

## Quilt Top Assembly

**1.** Referring to *Block Assembly Diagram* and to photograph for color placement, join 2 As, 2 Bs, 2 Cs, 2 Cs rev., 2 Ds, and 1 E as shown to make 1 fish block. Repeat to make 5 fish blocks.

**2.** Referring to *Quilt Top Assembly Diagram*, join fish blocks with turquoise/black and turquoise/purple Es as shown to complete quilt top.

**3.** Join 1½" x 22½" turquoise floral border strips to sides of quilt. Join remaining turquoise floral border strips to top and bottom of quilt, butting corners.

**4.** Join 2¾" x 30½" yellow/red dot border strips to sides of quilt. Join remaining yellow/red dot border strips to top and bottom of quilt, butting corners.

**5.** Join 5" x 35" pink print border strips to sides of quilt. Join remaining pink print border strips to top and bottom of quilt, butting corners.

## Happy Fish

### Finished Quilt Size
35½" x 43½"

### Number of Blocks and Finished Size
5 blocks        8" x 8"

### Fabric Requirements

| | |
|---|---|
| Pink print | 1⅛ yards |
| Yellow/red dot | ⅞ yard |
| Turquoise floral | ⅞ yard |
| Turquoise/black geometric | ⅜ yard |
| Turquoise/purple geometric | ⅜ yard |
| Bright prints for fish | scraps* |
| Backing | 3 yards |
| Red print for binding | ⅝ yard |

*Approximately 10" square each of 10 prints.

### Pieces to Cut

Pink print
    2 (5" x 36") borders
    2 (5" x 35") borders
Yellow/red dot
    2 (2¾" x 30½") borders
    2 (2¾" x 26½") borders
Turquoise floral
    2 (1½" x 28½") borders
    2 (1½" x 22½") borders
Turquoise/black geometric
    10 D
    7 (4½"–square) E**
Turquoise/purple geometric
    13 (4½"–square) E**
Bright prints for fish***
    10 A
    10 B
    10 C
    10 C rev.

**Rotary-cut Es; no pattern given.
***For each fish, cut 2 As from 1 fabric, 2 Bs from second fabric, and 2 Cs/2 Cs rev. from third fabric.

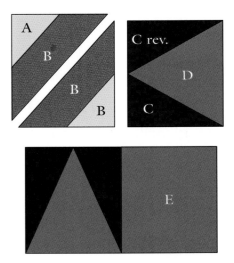

*Block Assembly Diagram*

## Quilting

Quilt in-the-ditch around all pieces. Quilt diagonal lines across quilt as shown in photograph. Or quilt as desired.

## Finished Edges

Bind with bias binding made from red print.

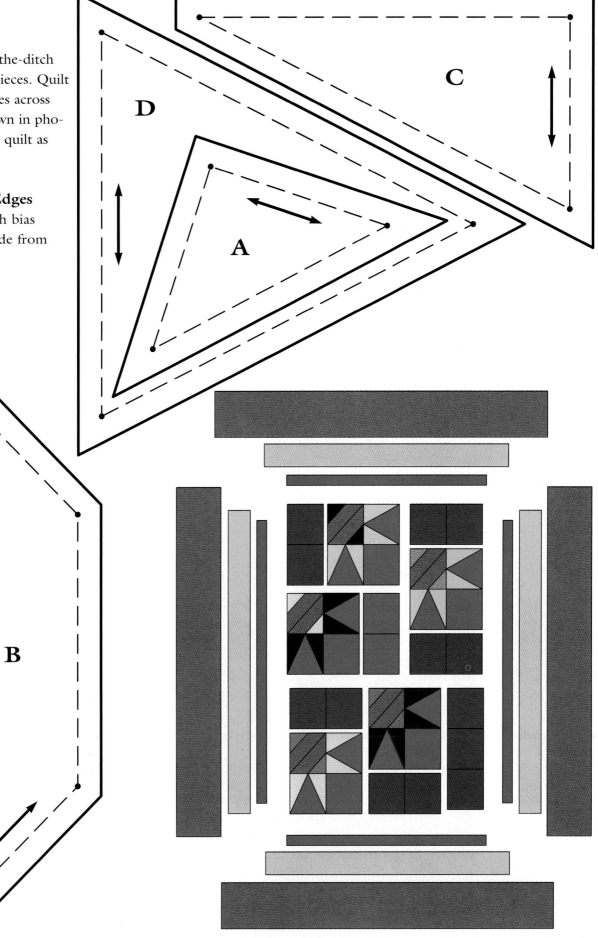

*Quilt Top Assembly Diagram*

# Quilts Across America

## Jane Haynes
Carlsbad, New Mexico

When Jane Haynes decided to learn quilting, she began by making a quilt and then throwing it away. "That wasn't a quilt I was proud of," she says. "It was made from old rags and it was lumpy and uneven. But now I wish I had kept it to show how much I've improved."

Jane made several more quilts

*"Quilting is the pattern God put in my life to hold me together."*

before she took formal quilting lessons. Now, after 20 years, she has finished many quilts and still has many to complete. "I figured that if I spent 3½ hours quilting every day," she says, "it would take me about 6½ years to finish every quilt top I own. And that's if I don't start any more in that time!"

## Charming Falling Dominoes
1995

This scrappy charmer is the second quilt Jane has made from her original design Falling Dominoes. "My guild exchanges friendship blocks each month, and I always try to design an original one," Jane says. As a single block, Falling Dominoes was symmetrical, but Jane realized that the corner curves could be turned in any direction. When set together, the resulting squares would create a winding path across the quilt. "Then I just doodled the design on graph paper," Jane says. "Collecting and coordinating all the fabrics took a *lot* longer!"

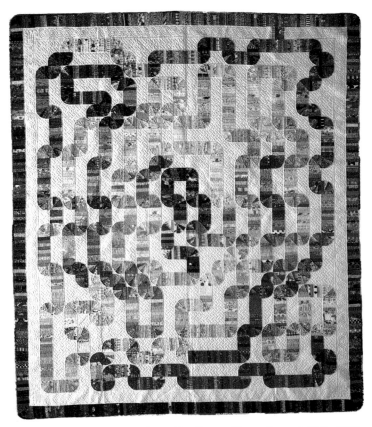

*To duplicate the look of Jane's quilt, first collect about 2,000 different fabrics! Jane sorted hers by color and value (light, medium, and dark) and carefully planned the placement of each before cutting and piecing.*

# Charming Falling Dominoes

## Finished Quilt Size
114" x 124"

## Number of Blocks and Finished Size
256 Block 1s    4" x 4"
292 Block 2s    4" x 4"

## Fabric Requirements
White    3½ yards
Prints    9¼ yards*
Backing    11 yards

*Jane used more than 2,300 prints in this quilt and needed only a scrap of each.

## Pieces to Cut
White
  2 (4½" x 118") borders
  2 (4½" x 106") borders
  214 (4½") squares
  252 C
Assorted prints
  1,290 (1½" x 4½") strips
  1,024 A
  256 B
  256 B rev.

## Quilt Top Assembly

**1.** Referring to *Block 1 Assembly Diagram*, join 4 As, 1 B, 1 B rev., and 1 C as shown to make 1 Block 1. Repeat to make 252 Block 1s.

**2.** Referring to *Block 2 Assembly Diagram*, join 4 (1½" x 4½") print strips along long edges as shown to make 1 Block 2. Repeat to make 182 Block 2s.

**3.** Referring to *Quilt Top Assembly Diagram* and to photograph for color arrangement, join Block 1s, Block 2s, and white 4½" squares in rows as shown.

**4.** Join rows. Join 4½" x 118" white border strips to sides of quilt. Join 4½" x 106" white border strips to top and bottom of quilt, mitering corners.

**5.** To make 1 side pieced border, make 29 Block 2s from print strips. Join blocks as shown in photograph. Join to 1 side of quilt. Repeat for remaining side border.

**6.** To make top pieced border, join 4 As, 1 B, and 1 B rev. to make 1 corner block. Repeat to make second corner block. From print strips, make 26 Block 2s and join blocks as shown in photograph. Join to top of quilt, butting corners. Repeat for bottom border.

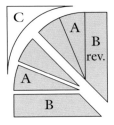

*Block 1 Assembly Diagram*

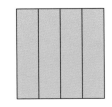

*Block 2 Assembly Diagram*

## Quilting

Quilt in-the-ditch around all pieces. In white squares, quilt 1" basketweave crosshatching as shown in photograph. Quilt cable in white border.

## Finished Edges

Bind with straight-grain binding made from remaining print strips.

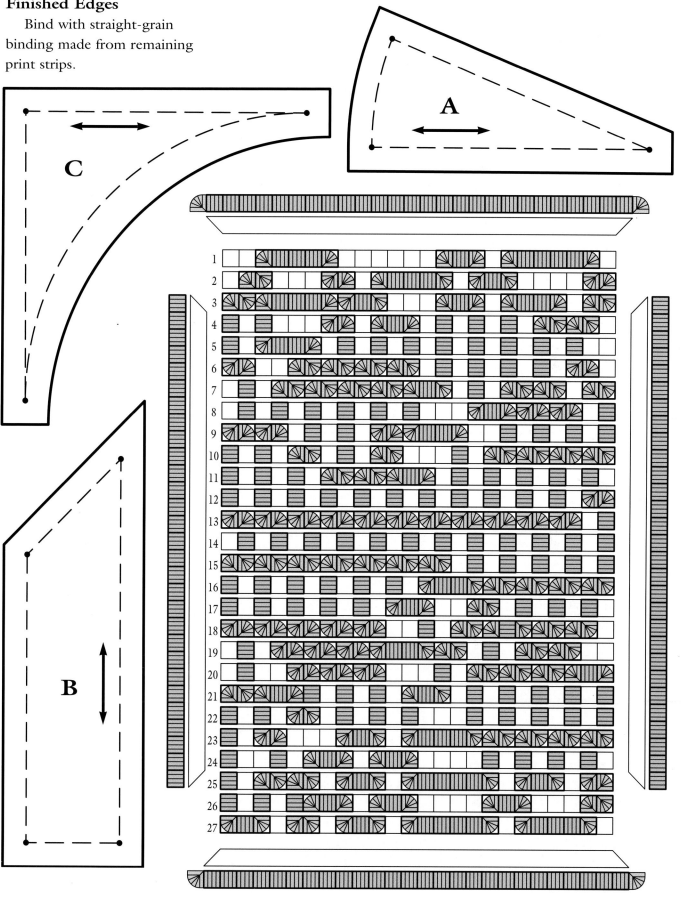

*Quilt Top Assembly Diagram*

# Jo Barry
## Portland, Oregon

"*In* this world of 'instant quick-and-easy,' I'm always amused when people ask me how long my quilts take to make," says Jo Barry. "I honestly don't know and don't really care!"

Although Jo's objective in her quiltmaking has always been top quality, she spent many years fitting quilting into the slivers of time left over from a busy life. "That meant one-block-a-day piecing and machine quilting," she says. Now that she is retired, she has the luxury of time to devote to her most fascinating pursuit. "So many things are satisfying—gardening, golf, travel, time with friends—and I do them all," she says. "But nothing is more rewarding than making something with fabric."

*"Quilting's the hobby I always wanted but never had time for."*

# Santa's Helpers
## 1994

"This is really *my* quilt," Jo says. "I've made quilts to give away, but this one was made for me."

Each of the Santa blocks was made for Jo by a member of her guild, the Northwest Quilters. Each is slightly different, reflecting the personality and sense of humor of the woman who made and signed it. "I thoroughly enjoyed the challenge of coming up with a setting to do justice to the blocks," Jo says.

The pieced corner blocks are Jo's own, designed after she saw an article on piecing picture blocks in an old issue of *Quilter's Newsletter Magazine*. The Santa is an old block, chosen to fit the traditional red and green color scheme she requested.

"The people who made the blocks are my dear friends," Jo says. "Each time I look at *Santa's Helpers*, I'm reminded of their creativity and talent, and how fortunate I am to be associated with them."

In these instructions, we offer two options. You may choose to piece the pictorial corners, as Jo Barry did, or use unpieced corner triangles of a bright Christmas print. Fabric requirements, cutting charts, and piecing diagrams for the corner blocks are on pages 50–52. For unpieced corner triangles, see instructions in Step 6.

## Santa's Helpers

### Finished Quilt Size
68" x 84½"

### Number of Blocks and Finished Size
22 Santa blocks    10" x 10"

### Fabric Requirements

| | |
|---|---|
| Red prints | 1¼ yards |
| White prints | 1 yard |
| Pink | ¼ yard |
| Black | ¾ yard |
| Green prints for Santa backgrounds | 1½ yards |
| Green print for borders | 2½ yards |
| Dark green | 2½ yards* |
| Gold lamé | ¼ yard |
| Backing | 5⅛ yards |
| Green print for binding | 1 yard |

*Includes ¾ yard for pieced or unpieced corner blocks.

### Other Materials

| | |
|---|---|
| Gold ribbon, ¼"-wide | 7½ yards |
| Red/green striped ribbon, 1¾"-wide | 5 yards |

## Pieces to Cut

Red prints**
   11 (3⅝") squares for A†
   22 E
   22 (1¾" x 5¾") G††
   22 H
   22 H rev.
   1 R

White prints
   22 B
   22 D
   22 (1⅛" x 5¾") F††
   44 (1½" x 2½") I††

Pink
   22 C

Black
   22 (1⅛" x 5¾") F††
   22 K
   22 K rev.

Green prints for Santas
   22 (2⅝") squares for J#
   22 L
   22 M
   22 M rev.

Green print for borders
   8 (8⅛" x 35¼") strips
   2 (8⅛" x 18") strips

Dark green
   2 (2" x 48") long sashing strips
   2 (2" x 46½") long sashing strips
   1 (10½") square
   2 (2" x 18") strips for side triangles
   24 N
   16 S

Gold lamé
   128 O
   16 (2"-square) P††
   1 Q
   1 Q rev.

**For each Santa, cut 1 A, 1 E, 1 G, 1 H, and 1 H rev. from 1 print.
†Cut each square in half diagonally for 22 As.
††Rotary-cut these pieces; no pattern given.
#Cut each square in half diagonally for 44 Js.

## Quilt Top Assembly

**1.** Referring to *Santa Block Assembly Diagram,* join 1 each of pieces A–E, 1 white print F, 1 black F, 1 G, 1 H, 1 H rev., 2 Is, 2 Js, 1 K, 1 K rev., 1 L, 1 M, and 1 M rev. as shown to make 1 Santa Block. Repeat to make 22.

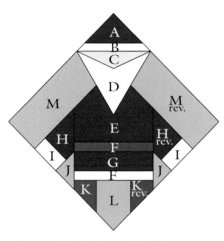

*Santa Block Assembly Diagram*

**2.** To make center gift block, fold 10½" dark green square into quarters diagonally; finger-press to form appliqué placement guidelines. Unfold. Appliqué 1 red print R to center of square. Appliqué 1 Q and 1 Q rev. to top of R as shown in *Quilt Top Assembly Diagram.* Cut 1 (4½") length of gold ribbon; fold under ¼" on each end. Appliqué to block, following placement lines on pattern piece R and covering center of bow with ribbon.

**3.** To make 1 inner sashing strip, join 2 gold lamé Os to each end of 1 N. Repeat to make 24. To make 1 outer sashing strip, join 2 gold lamé Os to pointed end of 1 S. Repeat to make 16.

**4.** Join Santa blocks, gift block, sashing strips, and sashing squares (P) in diagonal rows as shown in *Quilt Top Assembly Diagram.* Join rows.

**5.** Add long sashing strips to edges of quilt top as shown in *Quilt Top Assembly Diagram.*

**6.** To make pieced corner blocks, refer to fabric requirements, cutting instructions, and piecing diagrams on pages 50–52. To make unpieced corner triangles, cut 2 (18⅜") squares from dark green; cut each square in half to form 4 corner triangles.

**7.** Cut 8 (20") lengths of 1¾"-wide striped ribbon. Join 1 length of ribbon to each side of 1 corner triangle as shown on *Quilt Top Assembly Diagram,* mitering corners. Join 1 (8⅛" x 35¼") green print border strip to each side of triangle, mitering corners. Trim excess border fabric to make 1 (34⅞") corner triangle. Repeat to make 4 corners.

**8.** To make 1 side triangle, cut 1 (18") length of striped ribbon. Join to 1 edge of 1 (8⅛" x 18") green print border strip. Join 1 (2" x 18")

*Quilt Top Assembly Diagram*

dark green strip to ribbon. From pieced strip, cut 45° triangle with sides of 12⅝" and base of 16⅝" (see photograph). Repeat to make 2.

**9.** Join side triangles and corner triangles to edges of quilt as shown in *Quilt Top Assembly Diagram.*

**10.** Referring to photograph for placement, appliqué gold ribbon over edges of dark green sashing strip.

## Quilting

Quilt 1" crosshatch pattern across entire quilt, or quilt as desired.

## Finished Edges

Bind with bias binding made from dark green.

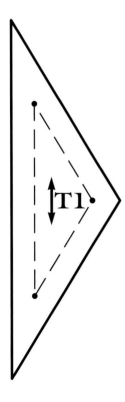

# Making Pieced Corner Blocks

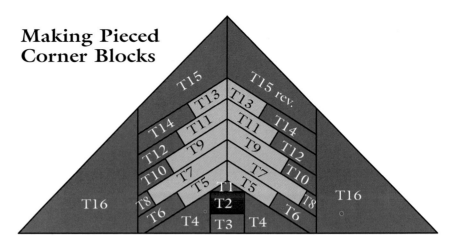

*Tree Piecing Diagram*

## Tree Block
## Fabric Requirements

| | |
|---|---|
| Red print | scrap |
| Green prints | ⅛ yard |
| Dark green | included with quilt |

## Pieces to Cut

| | | |
|---|---|---|
| T1: | use pattern | 1 green |
| T2: | 2½" x 1¾" | 1 red print |
| T3: | 2½" x 1⅝" | 1 green |
| T4: | half 3" x 5"* | 2 green |
| T5: | 1½" x 4" | 2 green print |
| T6: | 1½" x 3½" | 2 green |
| T7: | 1½" x 6½" | 2 green print |
| T8: | 1½" x 1¾" | 2 green |
| T9: | 1½" x 5" | 2 green print |
| T10: | 1½" x 3" | 2 green |
| T11: | 1½" x 4" | 2 green print |
| T12: | 1½" x 3¾" | 2 green |
| T13: | 1½" x 3¼" | 2 green print |
| T14: | 1½" x 4½" | 2 green |
| T15: | see Cutting Diagram | 1 green |
| T15 rev: | see Cutting Diagram | 1 green |
| T16: | half 8" square* | 2 green |

*Cut in half diagonally to make triangles.

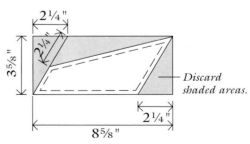

*Cutting Diagram for T15*

Cut 2 rectangles. With right sides facing, cut through both layers for 1 T15 and 1 T15 rev.

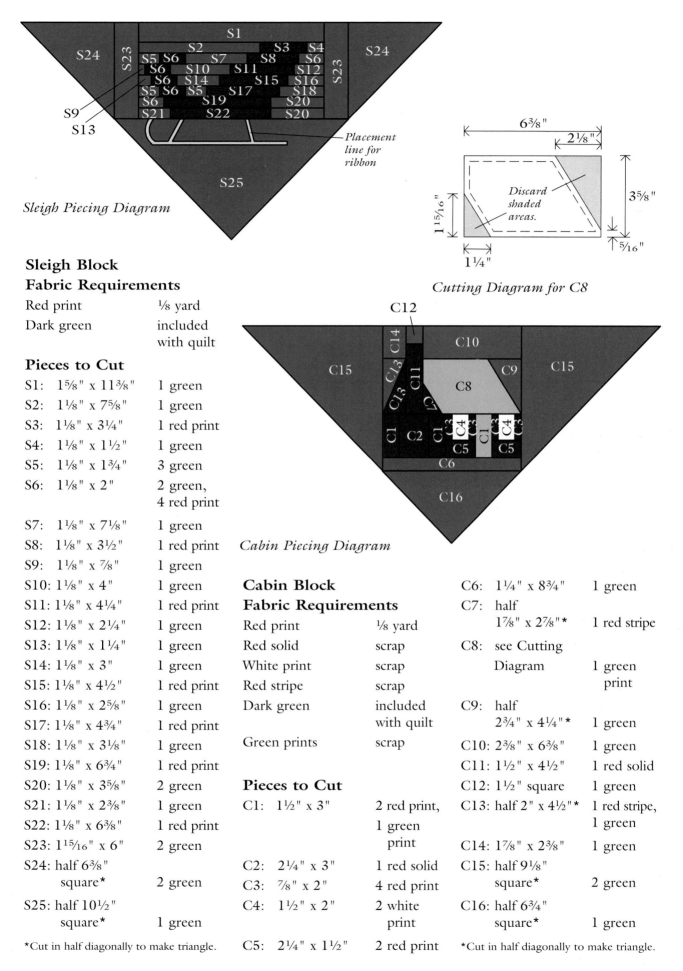

*Sleigh Piecing Diagram*

*Placement line for ribbon*

*Cutting Diagram for C8*

Discard shaded areas.

6⅜" · 2⅛" · 3⅝" · 1¹⁵/₁₆" · 1¼" · ⁵/₁₆"

*Cabin Piecing Diagram*

## Sleigh Block
### Fabric Requirements

| | |
|---|---|
| Red print | ⅛ yard |
| Dark green | included with quilt |

### Pieces to Cut

| | | |
|---|---|---|
| S1: | 1⅝" x 11⅜" | 1 green |
| S2: | 1⅛" x 7⅝" | 1 green |
| S3: | 1⅛" x 3¼" | 1 red print |
| S4: | 1⅛" x 1½" | 1 green |
| S5: | 1⅛" x 1¾" | 3 green |
| S6: | 1⅛" x 2" | 2 green, 4 red print |
| S7: | 1⅛" x 7⅛" | 1 green |
| S8: | 1⅛" x 3½" | 1 red print |
| S9: | 1⅛" x ⅞" | 1 green |
| S10: | 1⅛" x 4" | 1 green |
| S11: | 1⅛" x 4¼" | 1 red print |
| S12: | 1⅛" x 2¼" | 1 green |
| S13: | 1⅛" x 1¼" | 1 green |
| S14: | 1⅛" x 3" | 1 green |
| S15: | 1⅛" x 4½" | 1 red print |
| S16: | 1⅛" x 2⅝" | 1 green |
| S17: | 1⅛" x 4¾" | 1 red print |
| S18: | 1⅛" x 3⅛" | 1 green |
| S19: | 1⅛" x 6¾" | 1 red print |
| S20: | 1⅛" x 3⅝" | 2 green |
| S21: | 1⅛" x 2⅜" | 1 green |
| S22: | 1⅛" x 6⅜" | 1 red print |
| S23: | 1¹⁵/₁₆" x 6" | 2 green |
| S24: | half 6⅜" square* | 2 green |
| S25: | half 10½" square* | 1 green |

*Cut in half diagonally to make triangle.

## Cabin Block
### Fabric Requirements

| | |
|---|---|
| Red print | ⅛ yard |
| Red solid | scrap |
| White print | scrap |
| Red stripe | scrap |
| Dark green | included with quilt |
| Green prints | scrap |

### Pieces to Cut

| | | |
|---|---|---|
| C1: | 1½" x 3" | 2 red print, 1 green print |
| C2: | 2¼" x 3" | 1 red solid |
| C3: | ⅞" x 2" | 4 red print |
| C4: | 1½" x 2" | 2 white print |
| C5: | 2¼" x 1½" | 2 red print |
| C6: | 1¼" x 8¾" | 1 green |
| C7: | half 1⅞" x 2⅞"* | 1 red stripe |
| C8: | see Cutting Diagram | 1 green print |
| C9: | half 2¾" x 4¼"* | 1 green |
| C10: | 2⅜" x 6⅜" | 1 green |
| C11: | 1½" x 4½" | 1 red solid |
| C12: | 1½" square | 1 green |
| C13: | half 2" x 4½"* | 1 red stripe, 1 green |
| C14: | 1⅞" x 2⅜" | 1 green |
| C15: | half 9⅛" square* | 2 green |
| C16: | half 6¾" square* | 1 green |

*Cut in half diagonally to make triangle.

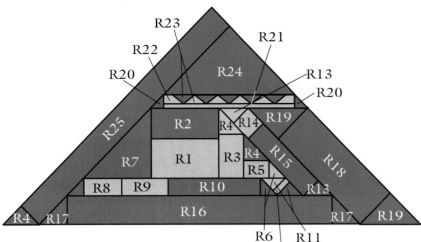

*Reindeer Piecing Diagram*

## Reindeer Block
## Fabric Requirements

| | |
|---|---|
| Brown | ⅛ yard |
| Dark brown | scrap |
| Dark green | included with quilt |

## Pieces to Cut

| | | |
|---|---|---|
| R1: | 2¾" x 4½" | 1 brown |
| R2: | 2¼" x 4½" | 1 green |
| R3: | 2" x 3" | 1 brown |
| R4: | half 2⅜" square* | 1 brown, 2 green |
| R5: | 1½" x 2" | 1 brown |
| R6: | half 1⅞" square* | 1 brown, 2 green |
| R7: | half 4⅞" square* | 1 green |
| R8: | 1½" x 2¾" | 1 green |
| R9: | 1½" x 3¼" | 1 brown |
| R10: | 1½" x 6" | 1 green |
| R11: | half 2" square* | 1 brown, 1 green |
| R12: | use pattern | 1 dark brown |

| | | |
|---|---|---|
| R13: | half 2⅛" square* | 1 brown, 1 green |
| R14: | 1¾" square | 1 brown |
| R15: | 1¾" x 5⅛" | 1 green |
| R16: | 2⅛" x 16¼" | 1 green |
| R17: | half 2½" square* | 2 green |
| R18: | 3" x 7⅜" | 1 green |
| R19: | half 3⅜" square* | 2 green |
| R20: | half 1⅝" square* | 2 green |
| R21: | ¾" x 7¹³⁄₁₆" | 1 dark brown |
| R22: | use pattern | 1 dark brown, 1 rev. dark brown |
| R23: | use pattern | 4 dark brown, 5 green |
| R24: | half 6⅜" square* | 1 green |
| R25: | 2" x 16½" | 1 green |

*Cut square in half diagonally to make triangle.

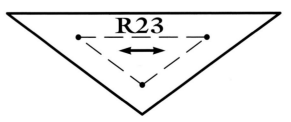

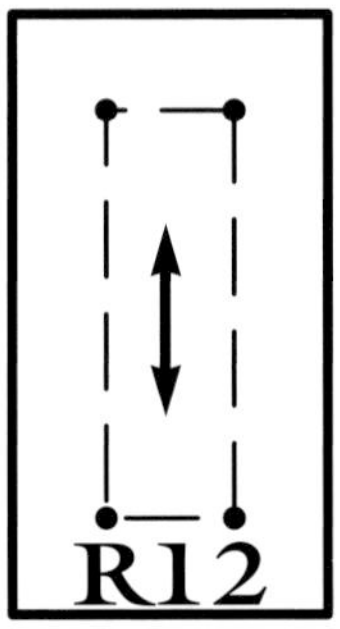

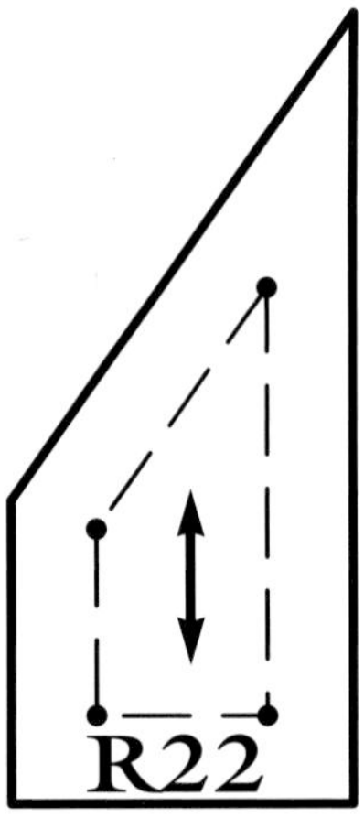

52

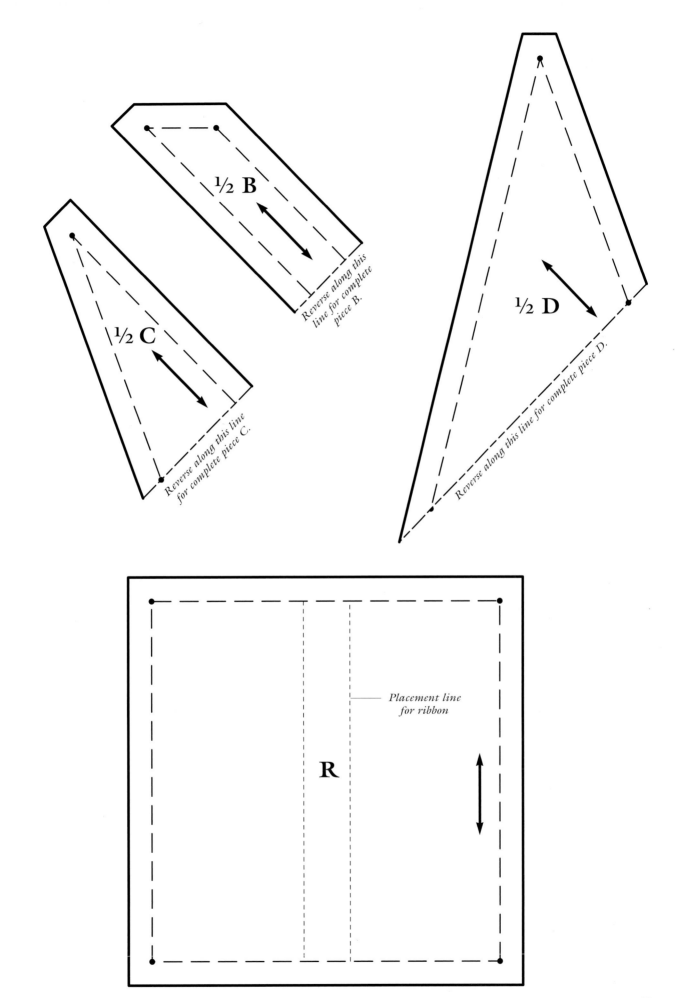

½ B

*Reverse along this line for complete piece B.*

½ C

*Reverse along this line for complete piece C.*

½ D

*Reverse along this line for complete piece D.*

R

*Placement line for ribbon*

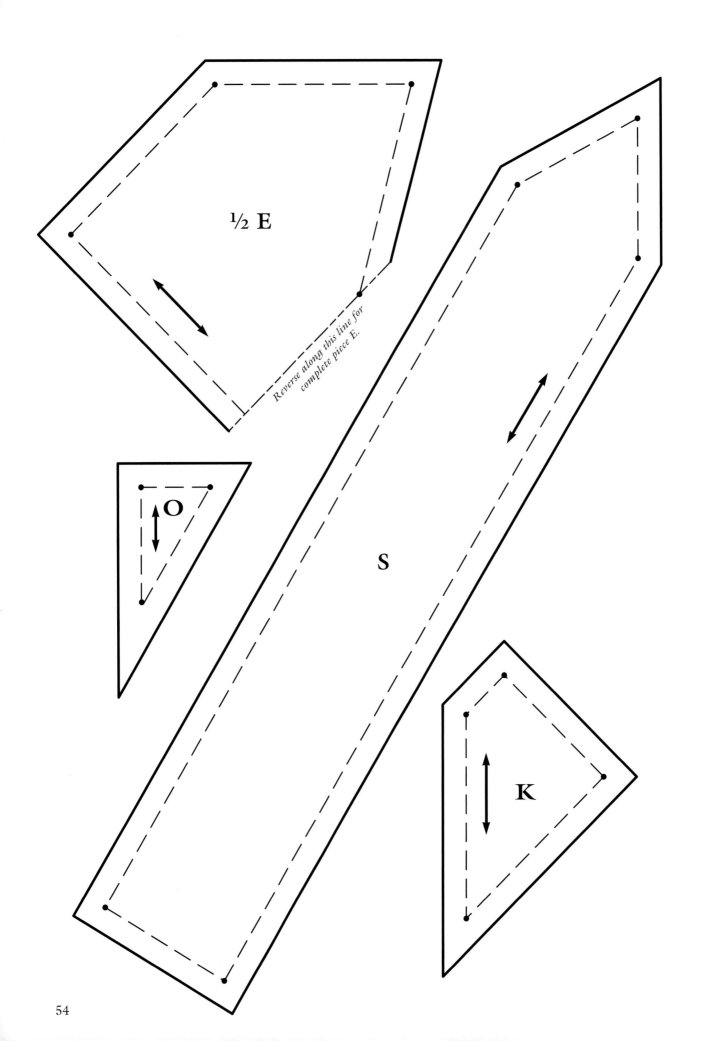

½ E

*Reverse along this line for*
*complete piece E.*

O

S

K

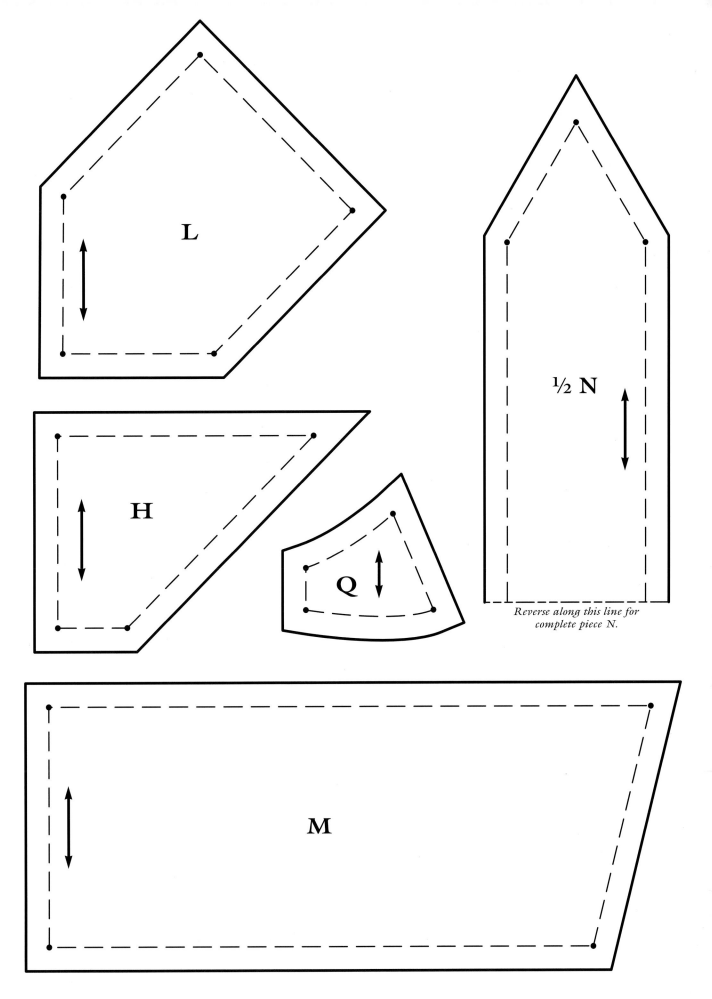

L

H

Q

½ N

*Reverse along this line for complete piece N.*

M

## Bette Haddon
New Port Richey, Florida

Quiltmaker Bette Haddon's studio is in a converted attic storeroom, a cozy space with a window overlooking the Gulf of Mexico. "When I first moved up here," she says, "I had to climb a ladder on the outside of the house to get in and out. The only access was through barn doors on the outside wall!"

Bette traces the beginnings of her love affair with quilting to her grandmother, who made a Grandmother's Flower Garden quilt for Bette's wedding many years ago. "I watched her spend

*"My best quilt is always the next one!"*

six months on that quilt," Bette says. "I saw the love, time, and even blood from pricked fingers that she spent on our gift." Although she had to put off quiltmaking until her children were no longer toddlers, Bette has worked passionately since then. "Quilting is many things to me," she says. "A creative endeavor, a source of satisfaction, and a gift of love."

## Cabin in the Woods
### 1994

*Cabin in the Woods* was the first full-size quilt Bette had made in about 15 years. She was working through a transition in the colors and patterns she used in her quilts, and she wanted to make something using brighter, primary colors. "I knew I wanted to make a scrap quilt with all the fabrics from my stash," she says. "The sky fabric was the uniting factor."

Bette used patterns from Janet Kime's book *Quilts to Share: Quick and Easy Quilts* as her starting point. (See "Resources," page 144.) She rotary-cut the pieces instead of using templates, a departure from the way she had always worked, and added the pieced border from strips left over from cutting. "For the back, I recycled a set of sunbleached cotton bedroom curtains," she says. "The uneven faded color is a look I found very interesting."

28 (1½" x 2½") L**
4 (1½"-square) S**
Red prints†
27 (5½" x 6½") A**
27 (2½" x 5½") B**
27 (1½" x 2½") C**
Gold prints†
27 (2½" x 4½") D**
7 (11¼") squares for E††

*Cut each square in half diagonally for 54 Fs.
**Rotary-cut these pieces; no pattern given.
†From each red print, cut 1 A, 1 B, and 1 C for each house. From each gold print, cut 1 D and 1 E for each house.
††Cut each square into quarters diagonally for 27 Es. (You will have 1 left over.)

## Quilt Top Assembly

**1.** Referring to *House 1 Block Assembly Diagram*, join 1 A, 1 B, 1 C, 1 D, 1 E, and 2 Fs as shown to make 1 House 1 Block. Repeat to make 15.

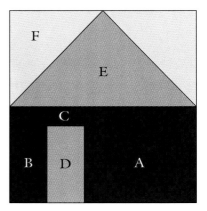

*House 1 Block Assembly Diagram Make 15.*

**2.** In same manner, join 1 A, 1 B, 1 C, 1 D, 1 E, and 2 Fs as shown in *House 2 Block Assembly Diagram* to make 1 House 2 Block. Repeat to make 12.

## Cabin in the Woods

### Finished Quilt Size
82" x 92"

### Number of Blocks and Finished Size
27 House blocks    10" x 10"
58 Tree blocks    5" x 10"

### Fabric Requirements

| | |
|---|---|
| Sky print | 2 yards |
| Green prints | 2¾ yards |
| Brown prints | ¼ yard |
| Red prints | 2 yards |
| Gold prints | 1¼ yards |
| Backing | 5 yards |
| Dark green for binding | 1 yard |

### Pieces to Cut
Sky print
27 (5⅞") squares for F*
52 (2½" x 3½") H**
56 (2½"-square) K**
8 (1½" x 2½") L**
14 (2½" x 5½") M**
14 N
14 N rev.
4 (5½"-square) R**
4 Q
4 Q rev.
Green prints
26 (5½" x 7½") G**
14 (5½" x 6½") J**
14 O
4 P
Brown prints
26 (1½" x 3½") I**

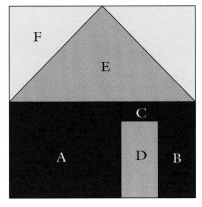

*House 2 Block Assembly Diagram*
*Make 12.*

**3.** Referring to *Tree 1 Block Assembly Diagram*, join 1 G, 2 Hs, and 1 I as shown to make 1 Tree 1 Block. Repeat to make 26.

*Tree 1 Block Assembly Diagram*
*Make 26.*

**4.** Join 1 J, 2 Ks, 1 brown print L, and 1 M as shown in *Tree 2 Block Assembly Diagram* to make 1 Tree 2 Block. Repeat to make 14.

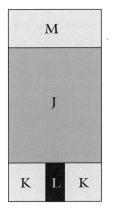

*Tree 2 Block Assembly Diagram*
*Make 14.*

**5.** Join 2 Ks, 1 brown print L, 1 O, 1 N, and 1 N rev. as shown in *Tree 3 Block Assembly Diagram* to make 1 Tree 3 Block. Repeat to make 14.

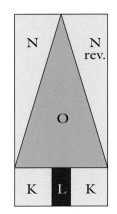

*Tree 3 Block Assembly Diagram*
*Make 14.*

**6.** Referring to *Tree 4 Block Assembly Diagram*, join 2 sky print Ls, 1 P, 1 Q, 1 Q rev., 1 R, and 1 S as shown to make 1 Tree 4 Block. Repeat to make 4.

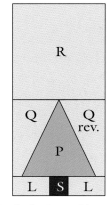

*Tree 4 Block Assembly Diagram*
*Make 4.*

**7.** Referring to *Quilt Top Assembly Diagram*, join house and tree blocks as shown into 8 horizontal rows. Join rows.

**8.** Cut remaining green, red, and gold prints into 1½"-wide strips of varying lengths. Join strips along short ends to make pieced border strips as follows: 2 (82½"-long) gold print strips, 2 (92½"-long)

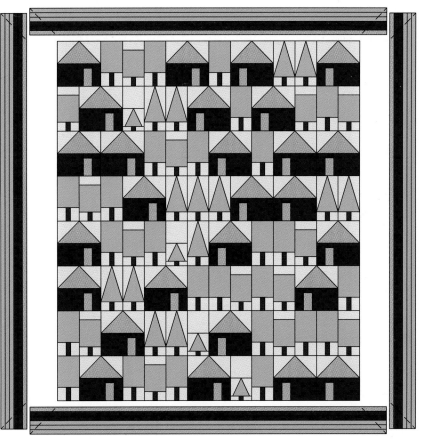

*Quilt Top Assembly Diagram*

gold print strips, 4 (82½"-long) red print strips, 4 (92½"-long) red print strips, 6 (82½"-long) green print strips, and 6 (92½"-long) green print strips.

**9.** To make top border, join 82½"-long pieced border strips in this order: 1 gold print, 2 red print, and 3 green print. Join to top of quilt with gold print strip innermost. Repeat for bottom border.

**10.** To make 1 side border, join 92½"-long pieced border strips in this order: 1 gold print, 2 red print, and 3 green print. Repeat to make second side border. Join to sides of quilt with gold print strips innermost. Miter corners.

## Quilting

Quilt 1" crosshatch pattern across entire quilt, or quilt as desired.

## Finished Edges

Bind with bias binding made from dark green.

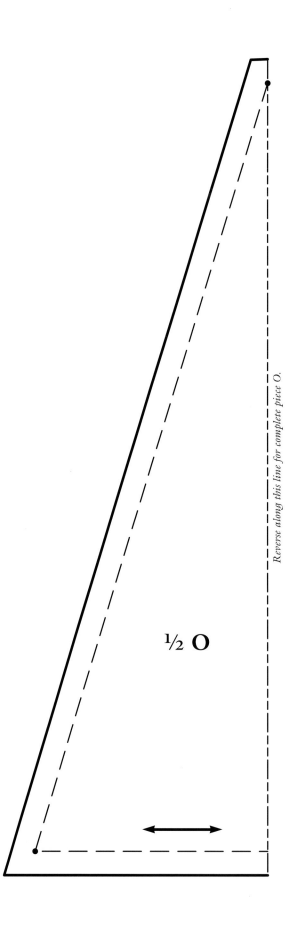

½ O

Reverse along this line for complete piece O.

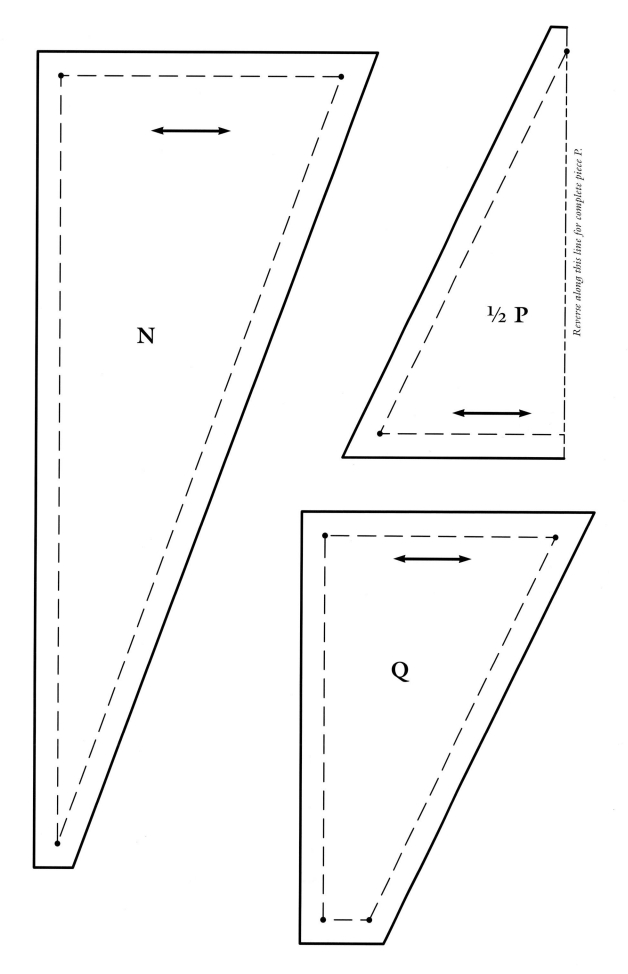

N

½ P

*Reverse along this line for complete piece P.*

Q

# Becky Herdle
## Rochester, New York

Becky Herdle learned to sew at an early age, but she did not become interested in quiltmaking until the 1970s. "My life revolved around my family and their activities—school, church, Scouts, and 4-H," she says. As part of her training as a 4-H leader, Becky took a class in basic quiltmaking that sparked her interest. A second course on

*"Quiltmaking is an exciting, constant challenge."*

machine piecing, taken just because she wanted to, provided the push that has kept her quilting to this day.

"Quiltmaking seems to have taken over my life!" she says. "Thanks to a very supportive husband, I've been able to concentrate on making quilts, teaching, and writing." In 1994, Becky's first book on quilting, *Time-Span Quilts: New Quilts from Old Tops*, was published by the American Quilter's Society. "Quiltmaking has been good to me and for me," she says. "It's a constant and exciting challenge."

# Red Lightning
## 1983

Becky's friend and fellow guild member, Suzzy Payne, asked Becky to make a quilt based on the traditional Hosanna pattern to illustrate her book *Creative American Quilts Inspired by the Bible.* "I realized the pattern had great potential if the blocks were arranged differently from the traditional

setting," Becky says. Using small block drawings on paper, she played with the setting until she found this pleasing arrangement. Since red is one of the colors of celebration in the Christian church, she chose to use red prints and solids for her quilt instead of the usual greens.

*Red Lightning* was also included in the 1985 *Quilt Art Engagement Calendar* published by the American Quilter's Society, and won an Honorable Mention ribbon at the 1983 National Quilting Association show.

42 C rev.

42 E

42 E rev.

42 G

42 G rev.

*Cut in half diagonally for 4 corner triangles.
**Cut into quarters diagonally for 50 setting triangles. (You will have 2 left over.)
†See Step 1.

## Quilt Top Assembly

**1.** Referring to *Cutting Diagram for H*, trim corners of each 16¼" x 4⅜" rectangle as shown to make 4 Hs. Set aside.

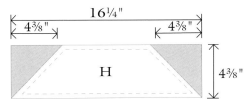

*Cutting Diagram for H*

**2.** Referring to *Block 1 Assembly Diagram*, join 1 white solid A, 1 red print B, 1 white solid C, 1 red print D, 1 white solid E, 1 red print F, and 1 white solid G as shown to form 1 pieced triangle. Repeat, using 1 white solid A and reversed pieces in same colors, to make second pieced triangle. Join triangles to complete 1 Block 1. Repeat to make 42 Block 1s.

# Red Lightning

## Finished Quilt Size
76¾" x 87¾"

## Number of Blocks and Finished Size
72 blocks        7¾" x 7¾"

## Fabric Requirements
| Red prints | 3 yards |
| Red solid | 5 yards |
| White prints | 2¼ yards |
| White solid | 3½ yards |
| Backing | 7 yards |
| Red solid for binding | ¾ yard |

## Pieces to Cut
Red prints
42 B
42 B rev.
42 D
42 D rev.
42 F

42 F rev.

Red solid
8 (8½") setting squares
2 (11⅞") squares*
13 (12¼") squares**
4 (16¼" x 4⅜") rectangles for H†
60 A
30 C
30 C rev.
30 E
30 E rev.
30 G
30 G rev.

White prints
30 B
30 B rev.
30 D
30 D rev.
30 F
30 F rev.

White solid
84 A
42 C

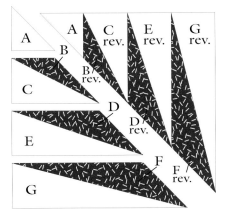

*Block 1 Assembly Diagram*
*Make 42.*

**3.** In same manner, join 1 red solid A, 1 white print B, 1 red solid C, 1 white print D, 1 red solid E, 1 white print F, and 1 red solid G to make 1 pieced triangle. Repeat, using 1 red solid A and reversed pieces in same colors, to make second pieced triangle as shown in *Block 2 Assembly Diagram*. Join triangles to complete 1 Block 2. Repeat to make 30 Block 2s.

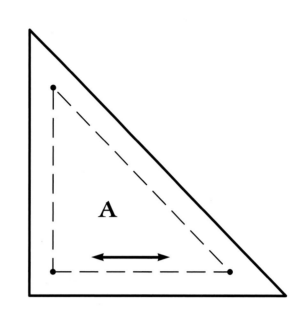

*Block 2 Assembly Diagram*
*Make 30.*

**4.** Join Block 1s, Block 2s, setting squares, setting triangles, Hs, and corner triangles as shown in *Quilt Top Assembly Diagram*.

## Quilting

Quilt around all pieces, ¼" inside seam lines, or quilt as desired.

## Finished Edges

Bind with bias binding made from red solid.

*Quilt Top Assembly Diagram*

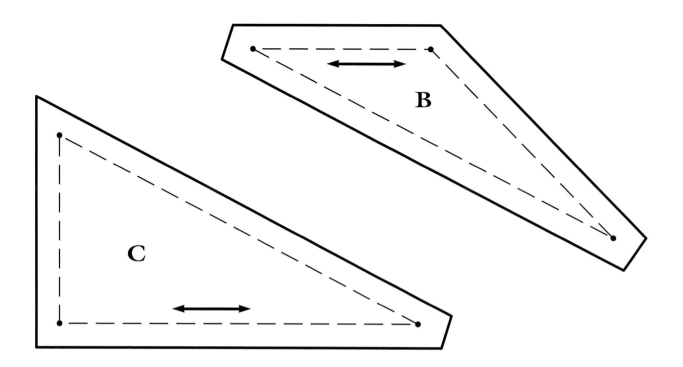

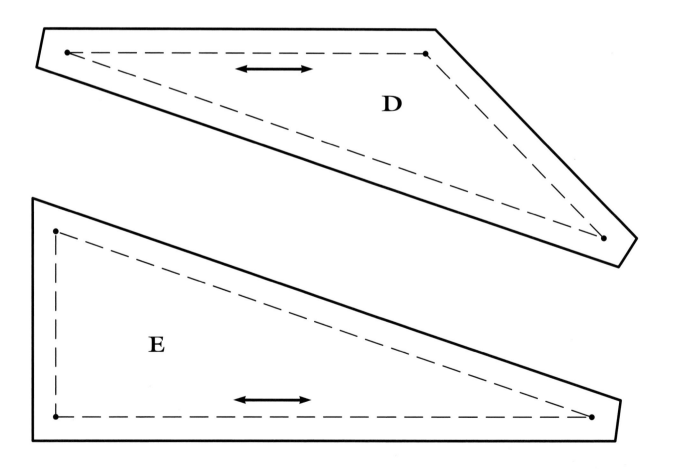

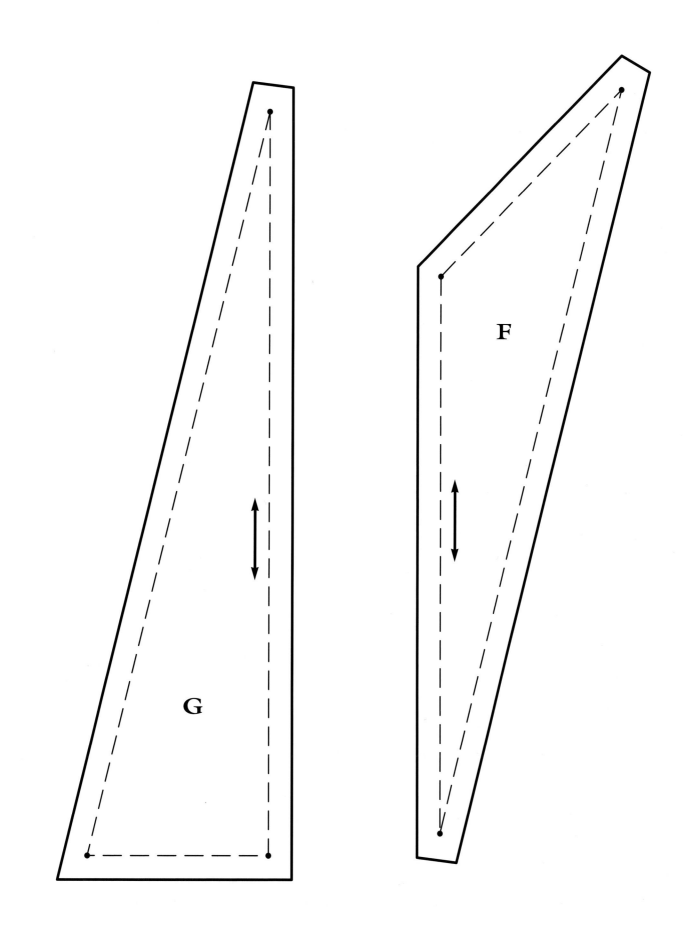

# Bobbi Finley
## San Jose, California

"I've always loved to fondle fabric," says Bobbi Finley. "When I discovered quilting, my love of sewing and my creative expression just came together."

Bobbi began quilting just a few years ago, after seeing antique quilts for sale and deciding she'd rather make one than buy it. She bought a quilt magazine, made one quilt using one of the patterns in it, and hasn't slowed down since.

Because of limited space, Bobbi usually makes small quilts, but her interpretations of traditional patterns have consistently won recognition for her pieces. The Museum of American Folk Art

*"Quilting lets me say I was here; this is who I was and what I did at the end of this century."*

in New York purchased one of her quilts for its permanent collection, and several of her wall hangings have been featured in books and magazines.

"Quilting makes me feel a part of the continuum of women past, present, and future," she says. "I'm leaving something of myself behind to say that I was here, at the end of a century and the start of a new millennium."

# Wasatch Memories
## 1994

"I don't know if it's because I'm an October child," says Bobbi Finley, "but autumn has always been my favorite season. Over the years I've collected leafy fabrics, knowing that someday I'd make an autumn quilt."

Bobbi lives in a part of California that has a Mediterranean-type climate; foliage here does not go through the distinct seasonal changes typical of most of the United States. So when autumn came without the annual show of leaves turning color, Bobbi decided to create her own.

From her collection of bronze and gold leaf fabrics, Bobbi pieced leaves in an original design based on the traditional Drunkard's Path. She appliquéd the border using a single rust/gold print, to help tie the diversity into a pleasing whole that reminded her of her former home near the Wasatch Mountains of Utah.

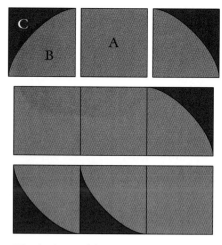

*Block Assembly Diagram*

## Wasatch Memories

### Finished Quilt Size
64" x 64"

### Number of Blocks and Finished Size
64 blocks      6" x 6"

### Fabric Requirements

| | |
|---|---|
| Leaf prints | 2⅝ yards |
| Dark brown print | 2¼ yards |
| Rust print | 2 yards |
| Light brown print | 1 yard |
| Rust/gold print | ⅝ yard |
| Backing | 4 yards |
| Dark brown for binding | ¾ yard |

### Pieces to Cut

Leaf prints*
  256 A
  320 B
Dark brown print
  2 (6½" x 62½")
    border strips

2 (6½" x 50½") border strips
320 C
Rust print
  2 (1½" x 48½") inner
    border strips
  2 (1½" x 50½") inner
    border strips
  2 (1½" x 62½") outer
    border strips
  2 (1½" x 64½") outer
    border strips
Rust/gold print
  20 D
  21 E
  27 F

*For each block, cut 4 As and 5 Bs of 1 leaf print.

### Quilt Top Assembly

**1.** Referring to *Block Assembly Diagram*, join 4 As, 5 Bs, and 5 Cs as shown to make 1 block. Repeat to make 64 blocks.

**2.** Arrange blocks in 8 rows of 8 blocks each, turning half of leaves to left and half to right as shown in *Quilt Top Assembly Diagram*. Join blocks into rows. Join rows.

**3.** Join 1½" x 48½" rust print border strips to top and bottom of quilt. Join 1½" x 50½" rust print border strips to sides of quilt, butting corners.

**4.** Join 6½" x 50½" dark brown print border strips to top and bottom of quilt. Join 6½" x 62½" dark brown print border strips to sides of quilt, butting corners.

**5.** Join 1½" x 62½" rust print border strips to top and bottom of quilt. Join 1½" x 64½" rust print border strips to sides of quilt, butting corners.

**6.** From light brown print, make 270" of 1¼"-wide continuous bias strip. Fold under ⅜" along each long edge; press. Cut 27 (3"-long) stems, 21 (3¾"-long) stems, and 20 (4½"-long) stems. Set stems aside. Referring to photograph for placement, pin remaining bias strip to dark brown print border for vine. Pin leaves and stems to border, matching 3"-long stems with Fs, 3¾"-long stems with Es, and 4½"-long stems with Ds. Appliqué in place.

## Quilting

Quilt around all pieced leaf blocks, ¼" inside seam lines. Quilt veins in pieced leaves. Quilt borders as desired.

## Finished Edges

Bind with bias binding made from dark brown print.

F

D

E

B

C

A

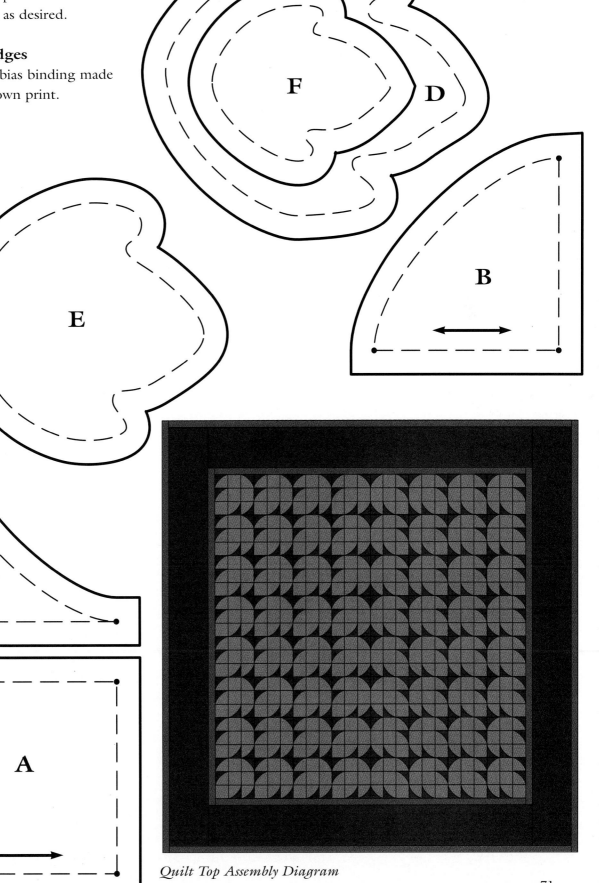

*Quilt Top Assembly Diagram*

# Traditions in Quilting

## Beth Crane Anderson
Plano, Texas

*Q*uilting provides a bit of much-needed continuity to Beth Anderson's nomadic life. "In the past 7½ years, my family has moved six times," Beth says.

"When my husband tells me we are being transferred again, the first thing I do is investigate the quilting

*"Quilting has given more to me than I will ever be able to give back."*

situation at our new location. I've found that if you are new to an area, quilters are the first to take you in and make you feel welcome."

Beth enjoys making traditional quilts in the style of the 1920s and 1930s, using bright, contemporary colors instead of pastels. "I like 'utility' quilting," she says of the coarse thread and relatively long stitches she uses in quilting her pieces. "It gives an old feel to my quilts, and it takes much less time to complete!"

## Henon's Tulip Garden
### 1994

"This quilt has a special place in my heart," Beth says. "I made it in memory of my Uncle Henon, who loved flowers and spent each year creating a beautiful garden."

Beth planned and made *Henon's Tulip Garden* while she was recuperating from surgery. "I had plenty of time to remember him and plant a

garden in fabric." She found a photograph of a quilt she liked in Mary Elizabeth Johnson's *A Garden of Quilts* (Oxmoor House, 1984), drafted the patterns, and started work.

*Henon's Tulip Garden* was Beth's first appliquéd quilt and her first using trapunto (quilted motifs lightly stuffed with batting).

## Henon's Tulip Garden

### Finished Quilt Size
72" x 101"

### Fabric Requirements

| | |
|---|---|
| White | 5¾ yards |
| Magenta | 2 yards |
| Pink | ⅛ yard |
| Lavender | ⅛ yard |
| Purple | ¼ yard |
| Light orange | ⅛ yard |
| Dark orange | ⅛ yard |
| Light yellow | ¼ yard |
| Dark yellow | ⅛ yard |
| Medium green | 1⅝ yards |
| Light green | ⅛ yard |
| Backing | 6¾ yards |
| Pink for binding | 1 yard |

### Pieces to Cut

White
  1 (34½" x 63½") rectangle
  2 (17½" x 63½") rectangles
  2 (17½" x 34½") rectangles
  4 (17½") corner squares
Magenta
  2 (2" x 72½") sashing strips
  2 (2" x 63") sashing strips
  4 (2" x 17½") sashing strips
  16 B
Pink
  16 A
Lavender
  12 A
Purple
  12 B
Light orange
  8 A
Dark orange
  8 B
Light yellow
  12 B
Dark yellow
  12 A

Medium green*
  44 C
  44 C rev.
Light green
  4 C
  4 C rev.
*See Step 1 before cutting.

### Quilt Top Assembly

**1.** From 20" square of medium green, make 450" of ¾"-wide continuous bias strip. Fold under ¼" on each long edge; press. Cut strip into stems as follows: 6 (21½") stems, 2 (14½") stems, 4 (12½") stems, 4 (10½") stems, 6 (8¾") stems, 8 (7½") stems, 4 (6½") stems, and 8 (5¾") stems. Set aside.

**2.** Referring to *Quilt Top Assembly Diagram*, join white rectangles, white squares, and magenta sashing strips as shown to complete quilt top.

**3.** Appliqué stems to quilt as shown in *Appliqué Placement Diagram*. Referring to photograph for placement, appliqué As and Bs to quilt, covering raw edges of stems. Appliqué Cs and Cs rev. as shown.

**4.** Round corners of quilt, as shown in photograph.

### Quilting

Quilt around all appliquéd stems, tulips, and leaves. Referring to photograph for placement and using templates A and B as patterns, quilt tulips and crossed tulips. Quilt remainder in 1½" crosshatch pattern.

### Finished Edges

Bind with bias binding made from pink.

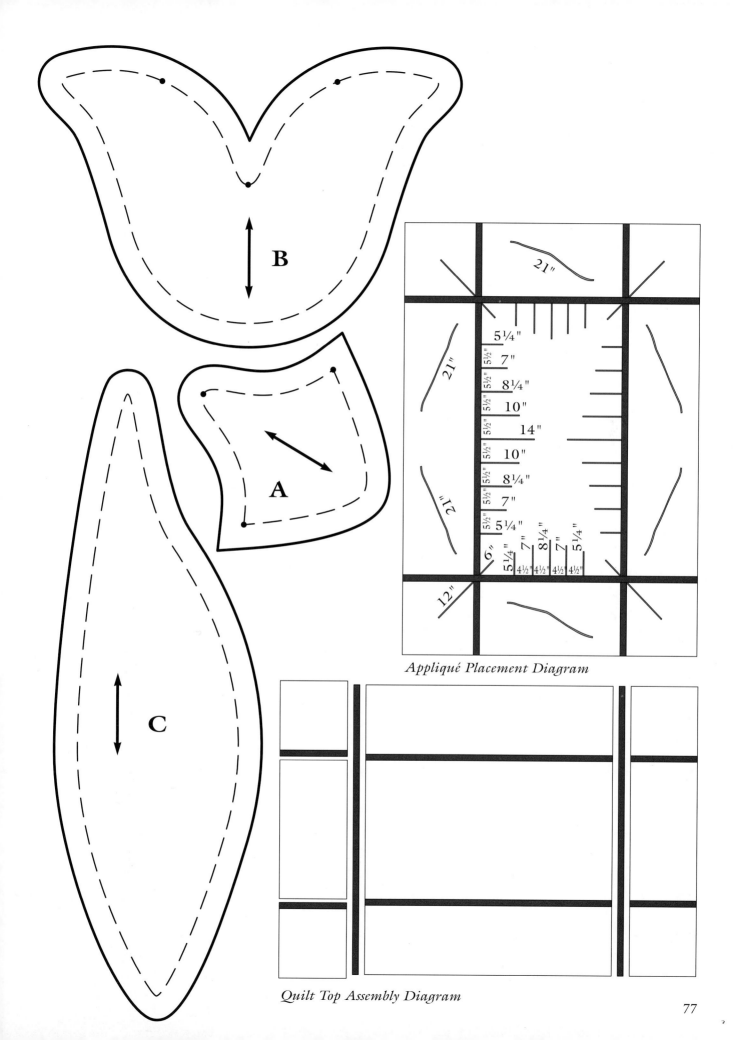

**B**

**A**

**C**

21"

21"

21"

5¼"
7"
8¼"
10"
14"
10"
8¼"
7"
5¼"

5½"
5½"
5½"
5½"
5½"
5½"
5½"
5½"

6"
5¼"
4½"
7"
4½"
8¼"
4½"
7"
4½"
5¼"

12"

*Appliqué Placement Diagram*

*Quilt Top Assembly Diagram*

# Ruth R. Easley
## Atlanta, Georgia

hile working at a church bazaar 14 years ago, Ruth Easley met a young woman eager to share her knowledge of quilting. The young quilter's enthusiasm sparked interest in several of the church members, and she organized a 6-week-long beginning class for them. "With her encouragement, I made my first appliquéd bed-size quilt," Ruth says.

Ruth became one of the charter members of the East Cobb Quilter's Guild in Marietta, a group that now numbers more than 200 and holds a widely-attended regional show every other year. A subgroup of the guild also exchanges visits with European quilters, and Ruth has visited with women in England, France, and the Netherlands.

"I've had the opportunity to meet and make many special friends," Ruth says. "Quilting is to enjoy, and I've certainly enjoyed the years I've spent quilting."

# Petronella's Garden
## 1989

One of the favorite activities of the East Cobb Quilter's Guild members is their block exchange program. Each member who wants to participate makes a block in an agreed-upon pattern and color scheme, and one of the participants wins all the blocks in a random drawing.

Ruth won 10 Petronella's Garden blocks in a drawing in late 1988. She made 12 more like the original 10, and then enlarged the original flower for the center block.

2 ($2\frac{1}{2}$" x $46\frac{3}{8}$") long
sashing strips

4 ($2\frac{1}{2}$" x $25\frac{1}{4}$") inner
border strips

4 ($2\frac{1}{2}$" x $43\frac{1}{4}$") inner
border strips

4 ($2\frac{1}{2}$" x $10\frac{1}{2}$") short
sashing strips

14 ($2\frac{3}{8}$" x $10\frac{1}{2}$") short
sashing strips

Green prints**

6 A

3 ($1\frac{1}{4}$" x 12") bias strips†

44 D

22 (1" x $8\frac{1}{2}$") bias strips†

Yellow print

3 C

22 F

Assorted prints

30 B

220 E

*Cut in half diagonally for 4 corner
triangles.
**For center block, cut As and 12" bias
strips from 1 green print. For each
flower block, cut 2 Ds and 1 ($8\frac{1}{2}$") bias
strip from 1 green print.
†Fold under $\frac{1}{4}$" along 1 end and each
long edge; press.

## Petronella's Garden

### Finished Quilt Size
70" x 82"

### Number of Blocks and Finished Size

| | |
|---|---|
| 1 Center Block | 20" x 20" |
| 12 Flower Blocks | 10" x 10" |
| 10 Flower Blocks | $9\frac{1}{4}$" x 10" |

### Fabric Requirements

| | |
|---|---|
| White | 4 yards |
| Green solid | $2\frac{1}{2}$ yards |
| Green prints | $\frac{3}{4}$ yard |
| Yellow print | $\frac{1}{2}$ yard |
| Assorted prints | 2 yards |
| Backing | $4\frac{1}{2}$ yards |
| Green solid for binding | $\frac{3}{4}$ yard |

### Pieces to Cut

White

4 ($7\frac{1}{2}$" x $39\frac{1}{4}$")
border strips

2 ($20\frac{7}{8}$") squares*

1 ($20\frac{1}{2}$") square

12 ($10\frac{1}{2}$") squares

10 ($9\frac{3}{4}$" x $10\frac{1}{2}$")
rectangles

Green solid

2 ($2\frac{1}{2}$" x $82\frac{1}{4}$") border strips

2 ($2\frac{1}{2}$" x $70\frac{3}{8}$") border strips

2 ($2\frac{1}{2}$" x $78\frac{1}{4}$") long
sashing strips

## Quilt Top Assembly

**1.** To make center block,
fold $20\frac{1}{2}$" white square into
quarters diagonally; finger-press
to form appliqué placement
guidelines. Unfold.

Referring to *Center Block
Appliqué Placement Diagram*,
appliqué 6 As and 12"-long
bias strips as shown to make
stems and leaves.

Join 10 assorted print Bs
along straight edges to form 1
flower. Appliqué flower to top
of 1 stem as shown. Appliqué 1
C over center of flower, covering raw edges of Bs. Repeat to
complete remaining flowers.

*Center Block Appliqué Placement Diagram*

**2.** Join 2½" x 25¼" green solid inner borders to edges of center block, mitering corners. Join 7½" x 39¼" white border strips to edges of quilt, mitering corners. Join 2½" x 43¼" green solid border strips to edges of quilt, mitering corners.

Referring to *Trimming Diagram*, trim corners of quilt as shown. Join white corner triangles to corners of quilt as shown in *Quilt Top Assembly Diagram*.

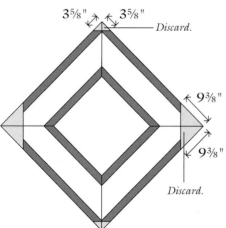

*Trimming Diagram*

**3.** To make 1 Flower Block, fold 1 (10½") white square into quarters diagonally; finger-press. Unfold. Referring to *Flower Block Appliqué Placement Diagram*, appliqué 2 Ds and 1

(8½") bias strip to square as shown. Join 10 Es along straight edges to form flower; appliqué flower to top of stem. Appliqué 1 F over center of flower to complete 1 Flower Block. Repeat to make 12 (10½") Flower Blocks.

In same manner, make 10 (9¾" x 10½") Flower Blocks.

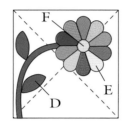

*Flower Block Appliqué Placement Diagram*

**4.** To make top row of quilt, join 4 (10½") Flower Blocks and

3 (2⅜" x 10½") sashing strips, alternating blocks and strips as shown in *Quilt Top Assembly Diagram*. Join 1 (2½" x 46⅜") sashing strip to bottom of row; join to top of quilt. Repeat to make and join bottom row. Join 2½" x 78¼" sashing strips to sides of quilt, butting corners.

**5.** To make 1 vertical side row, alternately join 5 (9¾" x 10½") Flower Blocks and 4 (2⅜" x 10½") sashing strips, beginning and ending with Flower Block. Join 1 (2½" x 10½") sashing strip to top and bottom of row. Join 1 (10½") Flower Block to top and bottom of row. Join to side of quilt. Repeat.

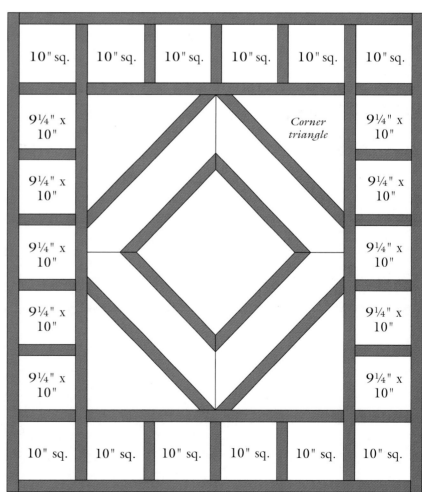

*Quilt Top Assembly Diagram*

**6.** Join 2½" x 70⅜" border strips to top and bottom of quilt. Join 2½" x 82¼" border strips to sides of quilt, butting corners.

## Quilting

Quilt around all flower petals, leaves, and stems. Quilt ¼" inside block seam lines. Stipple-quilt background of central block. Quilt *Border Pattern* in white border as shown in photograph; quilt background of border with 1½" crosshatch pattern. Quilt *Feather Wreath* and *Feather Bow* in each corner triangle as shown in photograph; quilt background of corner triangles with ¾" crosshatch pattern. Quilt cable pattern in green sashing strips and borders.

## Finished Edges

Bind with bias binding made from green solid.

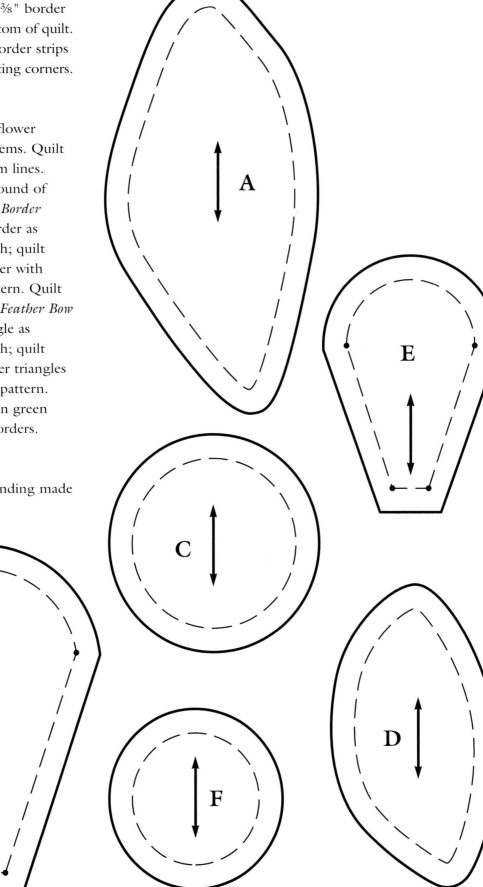

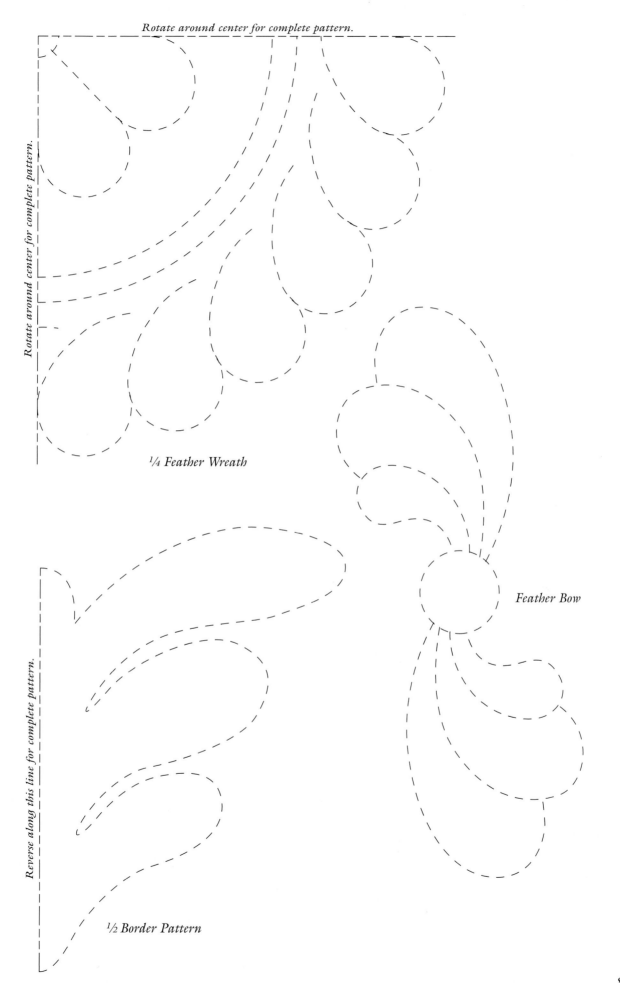

*Rotate around center for complete pattern.*

*Rotate around center for complete pattern.*

*¼ Feather Wreath*

*Feather Bow*

*Reverse along this line for complete pattern.*

*½ Border Pattern*

# Cindy Vermillion Hamilton
## Pagosa Springs, Colorado

"*I* enjoy so much creating something special and beautiful for the people I love," says Cindy Hamilton. "It's really exciting to imagine a great-grandchild I will never know getting to know me because of a quilt I made."

Cindy enjoys designing, drawing on her extensive knowledge of antique quilts for ideas.

*"Quilting has carried me through some rough passages and been part of my life's celebration."*

"I like making medallion quilts with both piecing and appliqué, and I like to use as many different fabrics as possible," she says. "I love the glorious fabrics available for quilters now." She does most of the work on her quilts, from appliqué to piecing to quilting, by hand. "Sometimes I join strips on the machine," she says, "but piecing and quilting by hand are some of the most relaxing things I do."

## Patrick's Pomegranates
### 1995

Cindy's love of antique patterns and bright colors reflects her years of study of historical quilts. "I discovered quilting on my own," she says. "I knew no one who could teach me, so I truly learned the hard way. As I studied the few books available, I was struck by the vivid colors used by the Pennsylvania Dutch in their quilts."

Cindy began appliquéing these Pomegranate blocks in bright colors in 1985 after seeing a photograph of an antique Pomegranate quilt in Mary Elizabeth Johnson's *A Garden of Quilts* (Oxmoor House, 1984). She completed the top and set it aside to quilt at a later time. "Then, in 1994," she says, "my newly married daughter chose this top for her husband because he loves bright colors. I designed the quilting patterns and finished the quilt in time to present Patrick with his Pomegranates for Christmas of 1995."

## Quilt Top Assembly

**1.** Fold 1 (29½") orange square into quarters diagonally; finger-press to form appliqué placement guidelines. Unfold.

Referring to *Appliqué Placement Diagram*, center 1 stem on square along diagonal placement line as shown; pin. Pin second stem along opposite diagonal, crossing first stem at center. Arrange 4 Gs and 4 Hs along stems as shown, tucking raw edges of leaves under stem. Appliqué stems and leaves.

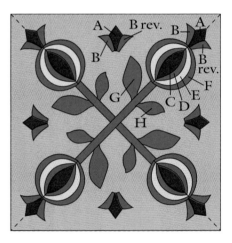

*Appliqué Placement Diagram*

**2.** Make 4 pomegranates (see Quilt Smart on page 88).

**3.** To complete 1 block, appliqué 4 As, 4 Bs, and 4 Bs rev. to make crowns midway between pomegranates, as shown in *Appliqué Placement Diagram*.

**4.** Repeat steps 1, 2, and 3 to make 4 blocks.

**5.** Join 2 blocks and 1 (6½" x 29½") sashing strip to make 1 vertical row as shown in *Quilt Top Assembly Diagram*. Repeat to make second row. Join rows with 6½" x 64½" sashing strip.

## Patrick's Pomegranates

### Finished Quilt Size
92" x 92"

### Number of Blocks and Finished Size
4 blocks          29" x 29"

### Fabric Requirements
| | |
|---|---|
| Orange | 7¼ yards |
| Green | 2¼ yards |
| Red | 1¾ yards |
| Yellow | ¾ yard |
| Backing | 8½ yards |
| Red for binding | 1 yard |

### Pieces to Cut
Orange
- 4 (29½") squares
- 2 (4½" x 92½") borders
- 2 (4½" x 84½") borders
- 2 (4½" x 72½") borders
- 2 (4½" x 64½") borders
- 1 (6½" x 64½") sashing strip
- 2 (6½" x 29½") sashing strips
- 104 (3⅞") squares for J*

Green
- 8 (1½" x 15½") stems**
- 32 B
- 32 B rev.
- 32 D
- 32 F
- 16 G
- 16 H

Red
- 32 A
- 16 C
- 8 (4¾"-square) I
- 22 (7¼") squares for K†

Yellow
- 32 E

*Cut each square in half diagonally for 208 Js.
**Press under ¼" on each long side.
†Cut each square into quarters diagonally for 88 Ks.

**6.** Join 4½" x 64½" border strips to top and bottom of quilt. Join 4½" x 72½" border strips to sides of quilt, butting corners.

**7.** To make top pieced border, join 1 I and 4 Js to make 1 pieced square. Join 2 Js and 1 K to make 1 Flying Geese unit; repeat to make 22 units. Join pieced square and Flying Geese units as shown in *Quilt Top Assembly Diagram*, turning half of geese to left and half to right. Join to top of quilt. Repeat for bottom border.

**8.** To make 1 side pieced border, make 3 pieced squares and 22 Flying Geese units. Join as shown in *Quilt Top Assembly Diagram*. Repeat for second side pieced border. Join to sides of quilt, butting corners.

**9.** Join 4½" x 84¼" border strips to top and bottom of quilt. Join 4½" x 92½" border strips to sides of quilt, butting corners.

**Quilting**

Quilt around appliquéd pieces, Flying Geese, and pieced squares. Quilt block backgrounds in ½" chevron pattern as shown in photograph. Quilt feather design in sashing and borders; or quilt as desired.

**Finished Edges**

Bind with bias binding made from red.

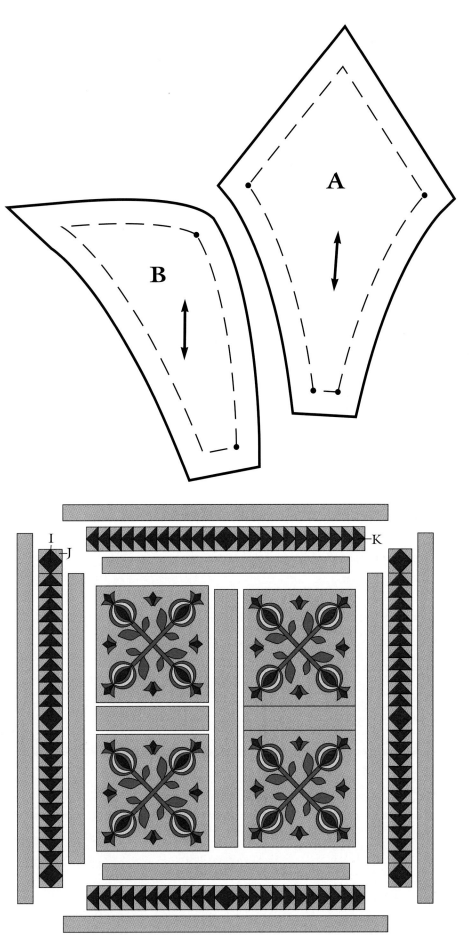

*Quilt Top Assembly Diagram*

# ❖ QUILT SMART ❖

Use either of the following methods to make the pomegranates. The appliqué method is a bit simpler, but you may find that the straight seams at the top and bottom of the pomegranate are easier to match by pre-piecing.

## Appliqué Method

At the end of 1 stem, arrange 1 A, 1 B, 1 B rev., 1 C, 2 Ds, 2 Es, and 2 Fs as shown in *Appliqué Placement Diagram*. Appliqué A, B, and B rev. to form "crown." Working from center of pomegranate outward, appliqué C, Ds, Es, and Fs, turning under seam allowances as stitching proceeds. Repeat to make remaining pomegranates.

Continue with Step 3.

## Pre-piecing Method

Appliqué 1 A, 1 B, and 1 B rev. to background as shown in *Appliqué Placement Diagram*.

Pin or baste 1 C at end of 1 stem as shown.

By hand or by machine, join 1 D, 1 E, and 1 F along curved edges to make 1 pieced half. Press seams to 1 side. Repeat. With right sides facing, join pieced halves along straight edges (*Figure 1*). Press seam to 1 side.

Center pre-pieced pomegranate over C. Appliqué inner and outer edges. Repeat to make remaining pomegranates.

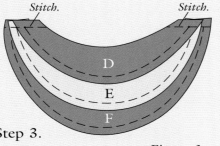

Continue with Step 3.

*Figure 1*

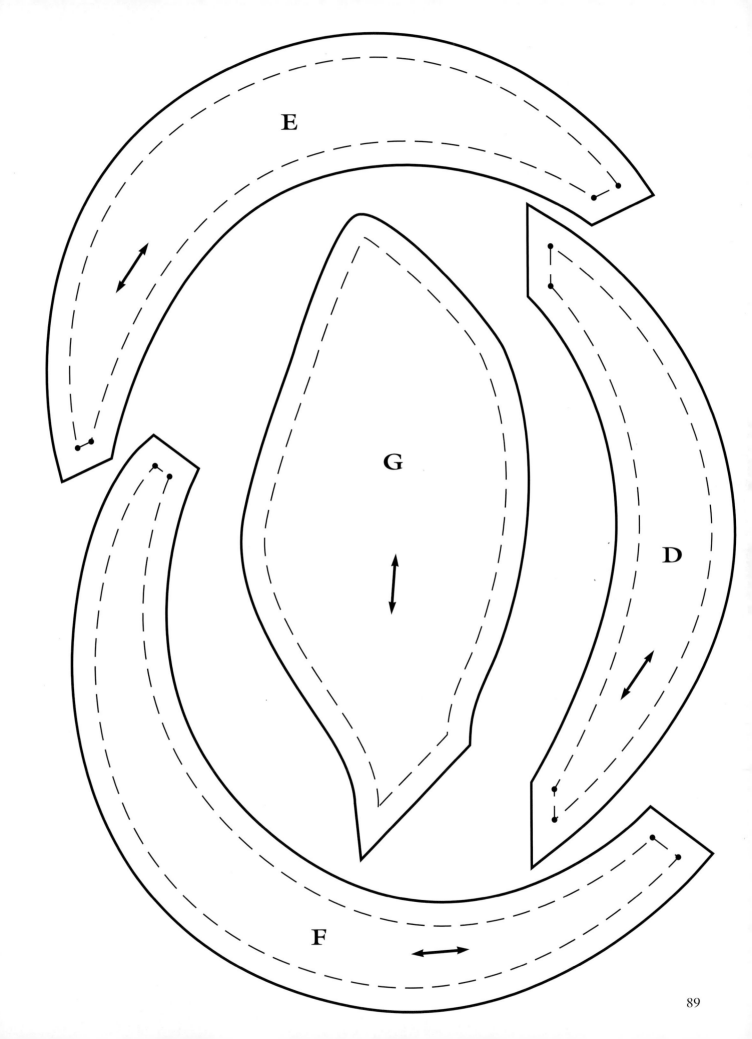

E

G

D

F

89

## Eula M. Long
### Salem, Oregon

"y initiation into quilting came at the right time to fill a void," says Eula Long. "My children were grown and I felt sort of lost."

Continuing the work she had begun in the community schools when her children were younger, Eula found that her organizing talents were still in demand. "They asked me to help establish a beginning

*"Quilting opened up a new dimension in my life."*

quilting class," she says. "Sixteen people signed up, and from these the Capitol Quilters club was formed." Her community activity now centers on quilting, as well. "The club members tie comforters for the homeless and demonstrate quilting at the local grade school. We're trying to keep interest in quilting alive."

## Basket Quilt
### 1994

For many years, Eula Long designed and made only pieced quilts, declaring that appliqué just "wasn't her thing."

"Then something wonderful happened," she says. "I went on a quilt cruise with Nancy Pearson, and I decided to give appliqué one more try. I have no idea what that teacher said or did, but I stepped off that boat a different person. I was hooked on appliqué!"

Eula soon branched into designing her own appliqué patterns. "I'm now working with flowers, baskets, and birds," she says. "I still love to appliqué, but my greatest pleasure comes from designing. So I just started designing and making the blocks for the *Basket Quilt,* and kept going until I had enough for a top!"

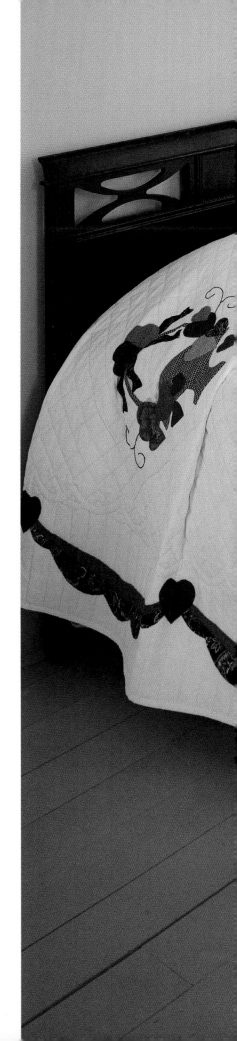

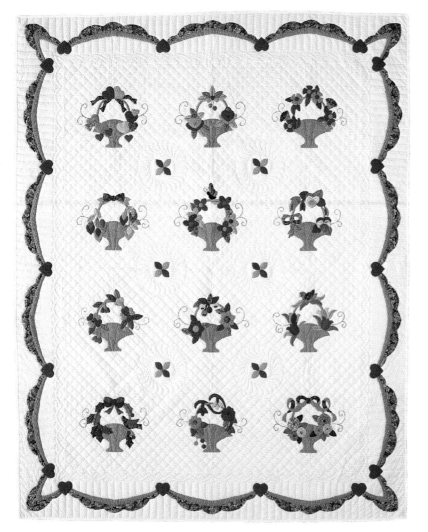

*In order to slightly reduce the number of pattern pieces required, the instructions for Blocks 4 and 6 use the bow shown for Block 10 instead of the individual bows Eula actually used.*

## Basket Quilt
### Finished Quilt Size
92" x 113"

### Number of Blocks and Finished Size
12 Basket blocks     15" x 15"

### Fabric Requirements
| | |
|---|---|
| White | 12 yards |
| Gray print | 1½ yards |
| Pink | 1¼ yards |
| Pink floral | 1¼ yards |
| Red | ¼ yard |
| Assorted solids and prints | 1 yard |
| Backing | 8⅜ yards |
| White for binding | 1 yard |

### Other Materials
| | |
|---|---|
| Black embroidery floss | 2 skeins |

### Pieces to Cut
White
  2 (14½" x 113⅜") borders
  2 (14½" x 92⅛") borders
  3 (22½") squares*
  18 (15½") squares
  2 (11½") squares**
Gray print†
  12 A
Pink
  12 R
  4 XX
  14 ZZ

Pink floral
  4 WW
  14 YY
Red
  18 B
  12 R

*Cut each square into quarters diagonally for 10 side triangles. (You will have 2 left over.)
**Cut each square in half diagonally for 4 corner triangles.
†See Step 2 before cutting pieces.

## Quilt Top Assembly
**1.** Fold each 15½" square into quarters horizontally and vertically to find center; finger-press. Unfold. Set 6 squares aside for setting blocks.

**2.** From 15" square of gray print, make 220" of ¾"-wide continuous bias strip. Fold under ¼" on each long edge; press. Cut strip into 12 (18") lengths for basket handles.

**3.** Referring to *Block 1 Appliqué Placement Diagram* and using finger-pressed center marks and *Guide for Basket Handle,* lightly mark position of basket handle on 12 white squares. Appliqué 1 (18") bias strip to each white square to form handle. Appliqué 1 A (basket) to each square as shown.

**4.** From assorted prints and solids, cut 2 (6½"-diameter) circles and 4 (4¼"-diameter) circles. (Refer to block in lower right-hand corner of photograph for color selection.) To make 1 yo-yo, turn under ¼" along edge of 1 circle. Make running stitches around circle through both layers. Pull thread tightly, gathering edges to center. Knot to secure thread. Center opening on front of circle, spread gathers evenly, and press yo-yo flat. Repeat to make remaining yo-yos. Set aside for Block 12.

**5.** From assorted prints and solids, cut 6 Bs, 6 Cs, 2 Ds, and 2 Ds rev. (Refer to upper left-hand block in photograph for color selection, or choose your own colors.) Referring to *Block 1 Appliqué Placement Diagram*, appliqué Bs, Cs, Ds, and Ds rev. over basket and handle to 1 block as shown.

**6.** Referring to *Appliqué Placement Diagrams*, cut number of remaining pieces indicated for each block. Appliqué over baskets and handles as shown to make Blocks 2–12.

**7.** Using 2 strands of floss, outline-stitch flourishes at edges of baskets and remaining embroidery details shown on each *Appliqué Placement Diagram*.

**8.** To make setting blocks, appliqué 2 pink Rs and 2 red Rs to center of 1 white square as shown in photograph. Repeat to make 6 setting blocks.

**9.** Join blocks, setting blocks, side triangles, and corner triangles in diagonal rows as shown in *Quilt Top Assembly Diagram*. Join rows.

**10.** Join 14½" x 113⅜" white borders to sides of quilt. Join 14½" x 92⅛" white borders to top and bottom of quilt, mitering corners.

**11.** Referring to *Border Appliqué Placement Diagram*, appliqué WWs, XXs, YYs, ZZs, and red Bs to border as shown.

## Quilting

Quilt around all appliquéd pieces. Quilt veins in leaves and 1" crosshatch pattern across baskets, as shown on *Appliqué Placement Diagrams*. In setting blocks, quilt feather wreath around appliquéd Rs. Quilt 2" crosshatch pattern across remainder of quilt. In borders, quilt parallel lines, 2" apart, as shown on photograph.

## Finished Edges

Bind with bias binding made from white.

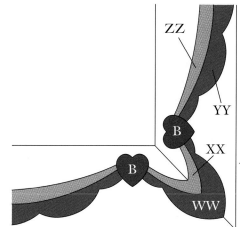

*Border Appliqué Placement Diagram*

*Quilt Top Assembly Diagram*

*Block 1 Appliqué Placement Diagram*

*Block 2 Appliqué Placement Diagram*

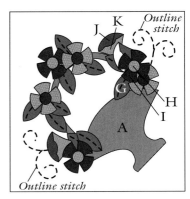

*Block 3 Appliqué Placement Diagram*

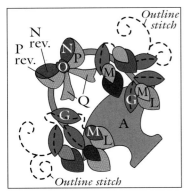

*Block 4 Appliqué Placement Diagram*

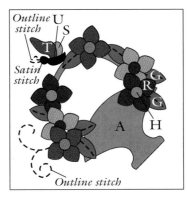

*Block 5 Appliqué Placement Diagram*

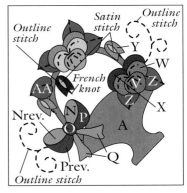

*Block 6 Appliqué Placement Diagram*

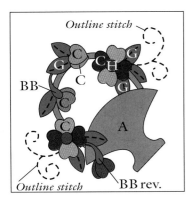

*Block 7 Appliqué Placement Diagram*

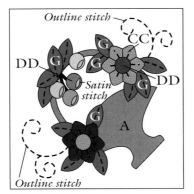

*Block 8 Appliqué Placement Diagram*

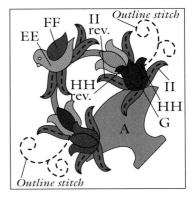

*Block 9 Appliqué Placement Diagram*

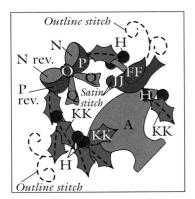

*Block 10 Appliqué Placement Diagram*

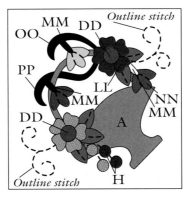

*Block 11 Appliqué Placement Diagram*

*Block 12 Appliqué Placement Diagram*

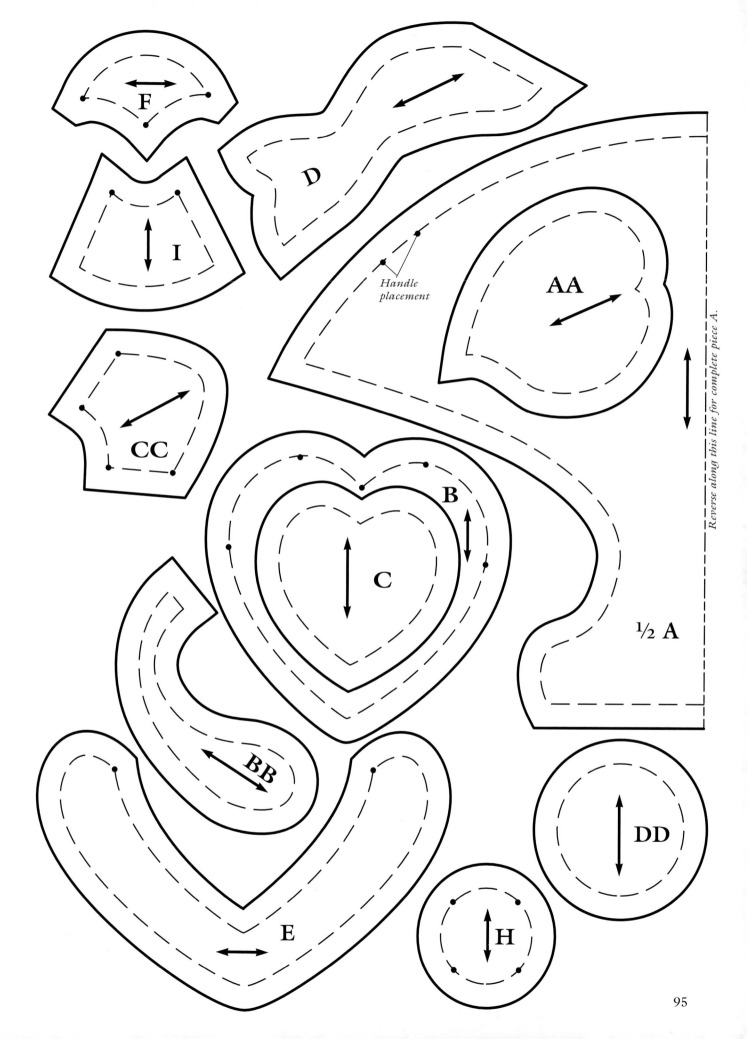

F

I

D

Handle placement

AA

CC

B

C

½ A

Reverse along this line for complete piece A.

BB

E

H

DD

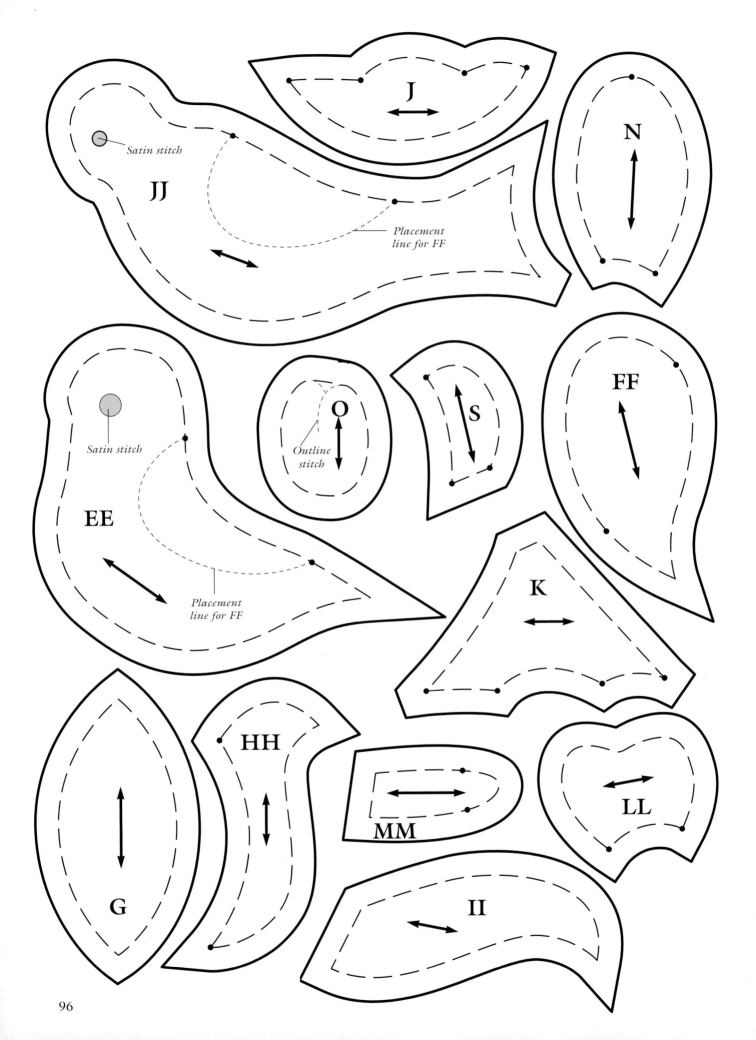

J

N

JJ
Satin stitch
Placement line for FF

EE
Satin stitch
Placement line for FF

O
Outline stitch

S

FF

K

G

HH

MM

LL

II

96

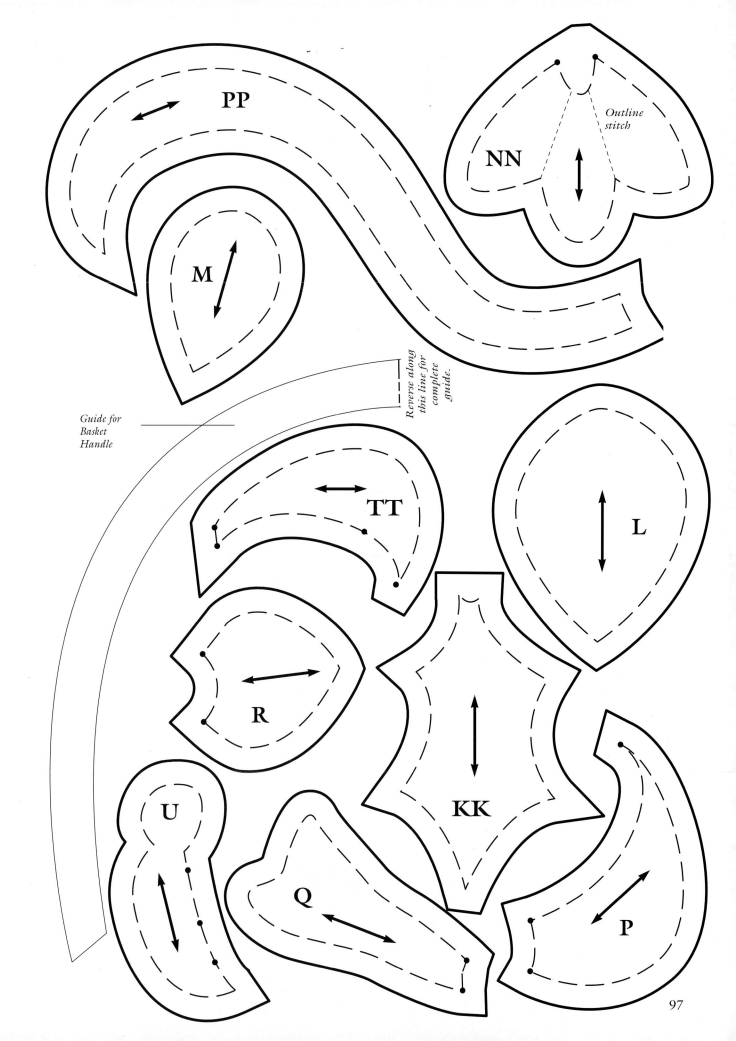

PP

NN

*Outline stitch*

M

*Reverse along this line for complete guide.*

*Guide for Basket Handle*

TT

L

R

KK

U

Q

P

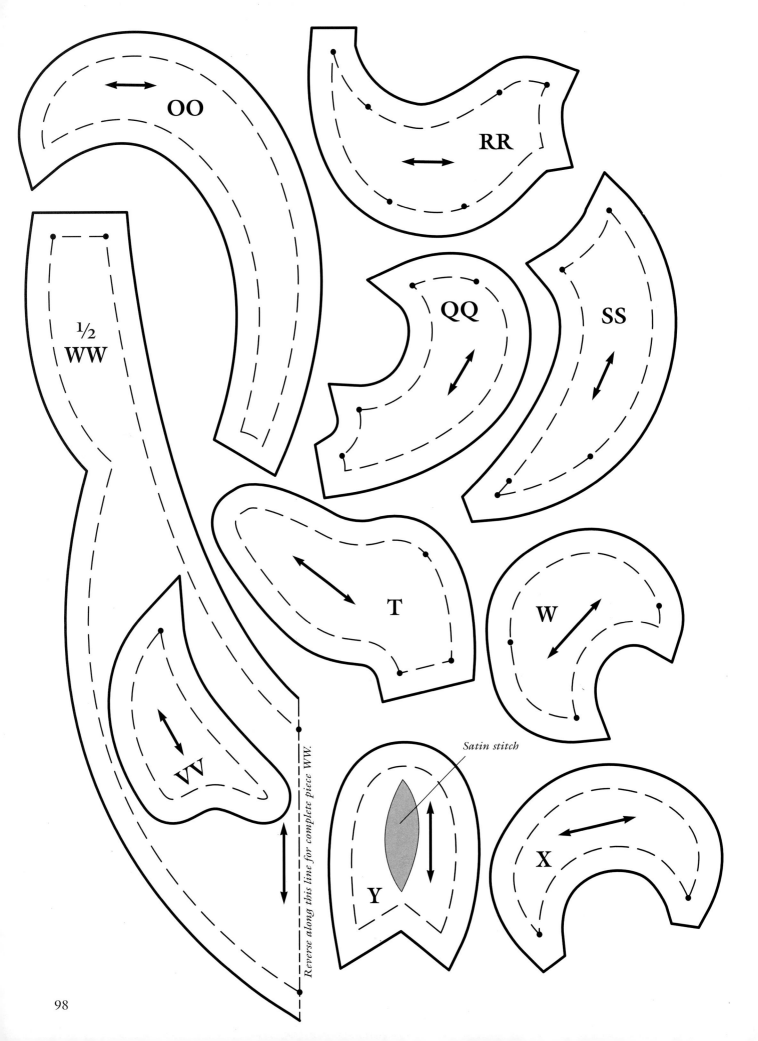

OO

RR

½ WW

QQ

SS

T

W

V

Satin stitch

Y

X

*Reverse along this line for complete piece WW.*

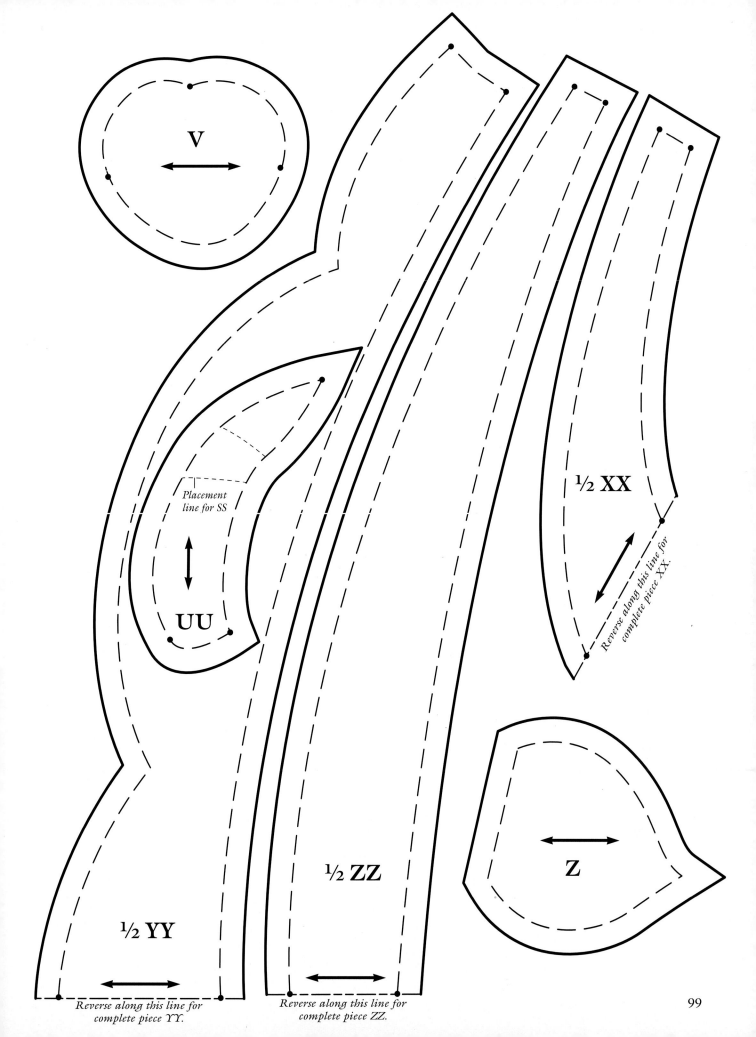

V

Placement line for SS

UU

½ XX

Reverse along this line for complete piece XX.

½ YY

½ ZZ

Z

*Reverse along this line for complete piece YY.*

*Reverse along this line for complete piece ZZ.*

99

# Linda Gibson
## Cumming, Iowa

"*I* grew up sleeping and dreaming under my grandmother's quilts," says Linda Gibson. "She died when I was only 2, but I feel a strong connection with her through my memories of those quilts."

To help make sure that other women's quilts don't become mere memories, Linda volunteers with a local historical society, assisting with conservation of the Mary Burton Collection of antique quilts. She has also become interested in quilt restoration and

*"So much of women's history is connected to quilts and textiles."*

would like to study textile conservation further. "I think there is a growing need for quilt restorers," she says. "People continue to be drawn to these textile works of art as they feel an increasing need to be connected to the past."

# Star Quilt
## 1993

"I love stars and scrap quilts," Linda says. "I use this quilt, one of my favorites, on my own bed."

Although the pattern is not an old one, Linda likes the fact that it looks like an antique. She has accentuated the resemblance through her choice of subdued, old-fashioned colors and prints.

*Star Quilt* has been shown at the Des Moines Area Quilters Guild Show and at the Iowa State Fair.

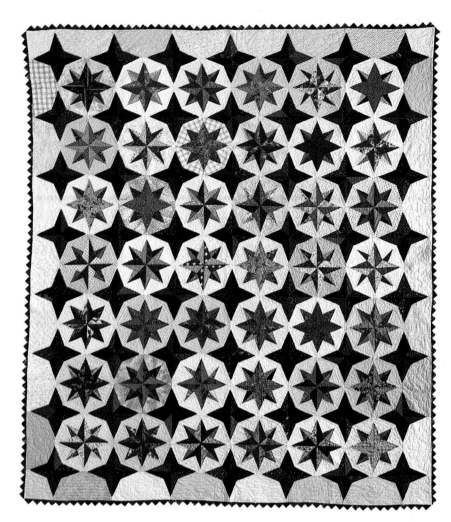

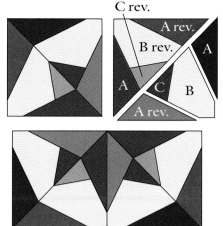

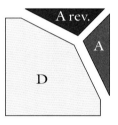

## Star Quilt

### Finished Quilt Size
91" x 104"

### Number of Blocks and Finished Size
42 blocks      13" x 13"

### Fabric Requirements

| | |
|---|---|
| Beige prints | 7¼ yards |
| Light prints | 2 yards |
| Medium prints | 2 yards |
| Dark prints | 7½ yards |
| Backing | 8¼ yards |

### Pieces to Cut

Beige prints
     168 B
     168 B rev.
     56 D

Light prints*
     168 A
     168 C
Medium prints*
     168 A rev.
     168 C rev.
Dark prints
     224 (6") squares**
     224 A
     224 A rev.

*For each block, cut matching pieces in sets of 4. See photograph.
**For prairie points.

### Quilt Top Assembly

**1.** Referring to *Star Block Assembly Diagram,* join 4 light print As, 4 medium print As rev., 4 dark print As, 4 dark print As rev., 4 Bs, 4 Bs rev., 4 Cs, and 4 Cs rev. as shown to make 1 star block. Repeat to make 42.

*Star Block Assembly Diagram*

*Border Block Assembly Diagram*

**2.** Referring to *Border Block Assembly Diagram,* join 1 dark print A, 1 dark print A rev., and 1 D as shown to make 1 border block. Repeat to make 56.

**3.** Join 6 star blocks to make 1 horizontal row. Join 2 border blocks with Ds adjacent, as shown on left end of second row in *Quilt Top Assembly Diagram.* Join to 1 end of row. Repeat for remaining end to complete row. Make 7 rows.

**4.** To make top border row, join 14 border blocks, rotating as shown on *Quilt Top Assembly Diagram.* Repeat to make bottom border row.

**5.** Join rows.

**6.** To make prairie point border, fold 59 dark print squares into quarters as shown in *Prairie Point Diagram.* Pin prairie points to 1 side of quilt top, aligning raw edges and overlapping points as required to fit edge of quilt. Baste. Repeat for opposite side. In same manner, make top and bottom borders using 53 squares each.

## Quilting

Quilt in-the-ditch around As and Cs. Inside dark stars formed at block corners, quilt ⅜" and 1" inside seam lines using contrasting thread. Quilt patterns given in each B, B rev., D, and D rev.

## Finished Edges

Fold backing of quilt away from edges; pin or baste in place. Using a ¼" seam, stitch around edges of quilt through prairie points, quilt top, and batting. Trim batting close to stitching. Fold prairie points out; press. Turn under ¼" along edge of backing and slipstitch backing in place.

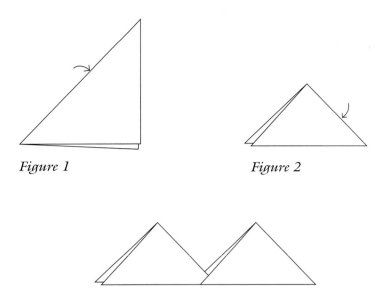

*Figure 1*          *Figure 2*

*Figure 3*

*Prairie Point Diagram*

*Quilt Top Assembly Diagram*

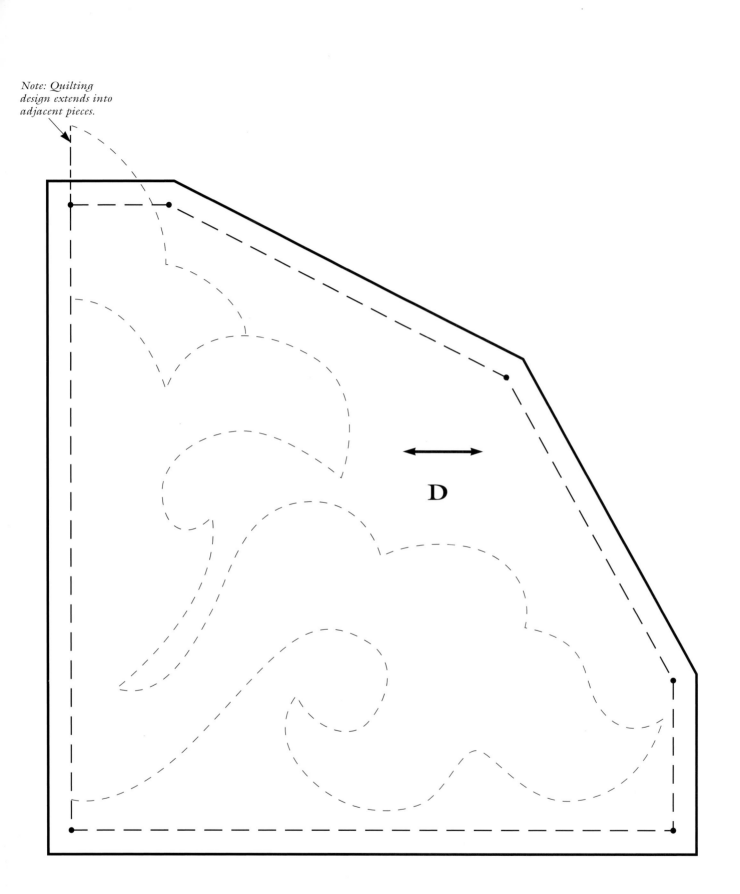

*Note: Quilting design extends into adjacent pieces.*

**D**

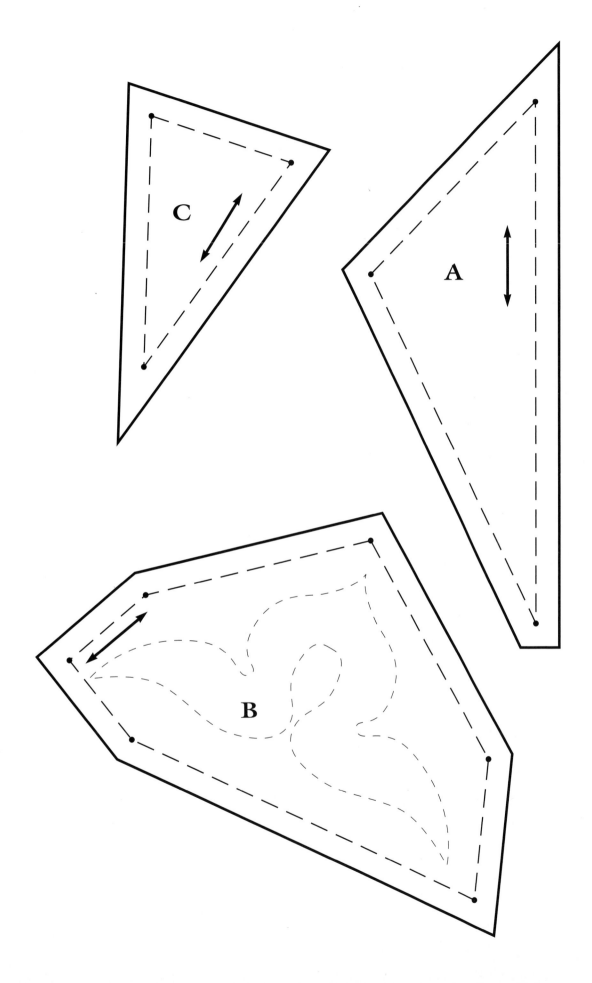

C

A

B

# Bee Quilters

Twilight

Granville Star

Springtime Jubilee

Prairie Queen

# Omaha Quilters' Guild
## Omaha, Nebraska

*These are the members of the Omaha Quilters' Guild who designed, pieced, and quilted* Twilight:
**Back row, l to r:** *Mary Ellen Poach, Gail Penkrot, Cindy Erickson, Joan Schoof, Gretchen Koziel.*
**Front row, l to r:** *Roma Seiker, Marge Anderson.*

The 400 members of the Omaha Quilters' Guild are serious quilters who enjoy sharing their craft. "We teach classes in schools, nursing homes, and adult education programs," says Roma Seiker, 1996 show chairman. "We also support the Children's Emergency Fund Project by making quilts for children who are patients at the University of Nebraska Medical Center and those who are victims of abuse or neglect." At Christmas, the guild members make stockings, collect toys, and raise money for gifts distributed to the needy by the Nebraska Department of Social Services.

"We also like to have fun sharing our work with each other," Roma says. "Show-and-tell is always the highlight of our monthly guild meetings!"

# Twilight
## 1995

This lovely quilt was designed and pieced by Roma Seiker and her mother, Marge Anderson, as the 1996 raffle quilt for the Omaha Quilters' Guild. "This is our main fund-raiser each year," Roma says. "The proceeds are used to further our educational programs and community projects."

Roma announced the winner on May 5, 1996, the finale of the guild's annual show. *Twilight* went home with Omaha resident Maureen Lubbers. "Although she is not a member of our guild, Maureen comes from a quilt-loving family," Roma says. "So we were delighted when her name was drawn. We know she'll love it always."

16 D

16 D rev.

Pink/purple print

  16 E

  16 F

Dark purple

  2 (6½" x 103") borders

  2 (6½" x 86") borders

  12 (6½" x 12½") strips

  17 (6½") squares

  16 E

Green print

  88 J

  4 K

Magenta

  12 (2½"-square) G†

  96 H

Assorted prints

  960 (2½"-square) G†

  112 H

  92 I

Purple solids

  124 L

**For rotary-cutting instructions for most pieces, see page 113.
† Rotary-cut these pieces.

## Twilight

### Finished Quilt Size
85½" x 102½"

### Number of Blocks and Finished Size
4 center blocks        12" x 12"

### Fabric Requirements

| | |
|---|---|
| Floral print | ¼ yard |
| Lavender | ⅛ yard |
| Purple print 1 | ¾ yard |
| Purple print 2 | ¼ yard |
| Pink/purple print | ¼ yard |
| Dark purple | 3¼ yards |
| Green print | ¾ yard |
| Magenta | ¼ yard |
| Assorted prints | 5½ yards |
| Purple solids | * |
| Light brown | ½ yard |
| Dark brown | ¾ yard |
| Backing | 7½ yards |
| Dark purple for binding | 1 yard |

*1 package of gradated solids in fat quarters. (See "Resources," page 144.)

### Pieces to Cut**

Floral print

  4 A

  16 C

Lavender

  16 B

Purple print 1

  32 B

  18 (2½"-square) G†

  144 H

Purple print 2

  16 B

## Quilt Top Assembly

**1.** From 15" square of light brown, make 231" of ¾"-wide continuous bias strip. From 20" square of dark brown, make 462" of ¾"-wide continuous bias strip. Fold under ¼" on each long edge of each strip; press. Cut light brown into 6 (38½"-long) vines. Cut dark brown into 12 (38½"-long) vines. Set vines aside.

**2.** Referring to *Center Block Assembly Diagram,* join 1 A, 4 lavender Bs, 8 purple print 1 Bs, 4 purple print 2 Bs, 4 Cs, 4 Ds, 4 Ds rev., 4 pink/purple print Es, 4 dark purple Es, and 4 pink/purple print Fs as shown to make 1 center block. Repeat to make 4.

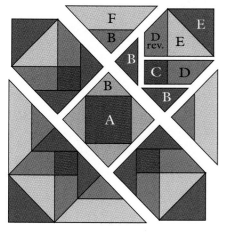

*Center Block Assembly Diagram*
*Make 4.*

**3.** Referring to *Quilt Top Assembly Diagram*, join center blocks with dark purple strips and 9 dark purple squares as shown to make central medallion.

**4.** Referring to *Block 1 Assembly Diagram*, join 5 assorted print Gs, 8 assorted print Hs, and 8 purple print 1 Hs as shown to make 1 purple Block 1. Repeat to make 14. In same manner, join 5 assorted print Gs, 8 assorted print Hs, and 8 magenta Hs as shown to make 1 magenta Block 1. Repeat to make 4.

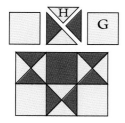

*Block 1 Assembly Diagram*
*Make 14 purple.*
*Make 4 magenta.*

**5.** Referring to *Block 2 Assembly Diagram*, join 4 assorted print Gs, 8 assorted print Hs, 8 purple print 1 Hs, and 1 assorted print I as shown to make 1 purple Block 2. Repeat to make 4. In same manner, make 8 magenta Block 2s.

*Block 2 Assembly Diagram*
*Make 4 purple.*
*Make 8 magenta.*

**6.** Referring to *Block Assembly Diagrams* for Blocks 3, 4, 5, and 6, join assorted print Gs and Is as shown to make 76 Block 3s, 16 Block 4s, 4 Block 5s, and 28 Block 6s.

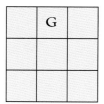

*Block 3 Assembly Diagram*
*Make 76.*

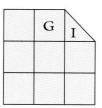

*Block 4 Assembly Diagram*
*Make 16.*

*Quilt Top Assembly Diagram*

111

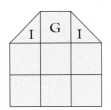

Block 5 Assembly Diagram
Make 4.

Block 6 Assembly Diagram
Make 28.

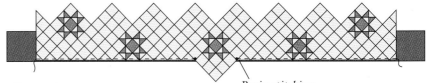

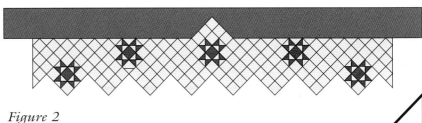

*Figure 1*

*Begin stitching.*

*Figure 2*
*Border Stitching Diagram*

**7.** Referring to photograph for color placement, arrange blocks, remaining purple squares, remaining Gs, Hs, and Is as shown in *Quilt Top Assembly Diagram*. Join blocks, squares, and triangles in diagonal rows as shown. Join rows.

**8.** To join top border, pin 1 (6½" x 86") border strip to top edge of quilt, leaving center squares free to extend into border, as shown on *Border Stitching Diagram, Figure 1*. Stitch from center of border toward each end. Press seam toward border. Press under ¼" on each raw edge of extension. Pull extension to right side as shown in *Figure 2*. Appliqué extension to border. If desired, turn border over and cut away fabric under extension.

**9.** Repeat to join remaining borders. Miter corners.

**10.** Referring to photograph for placement, appliqué bias vines across dark purple strips. Appliqué 4 Ks (small leaves) in corners of center dark purple square. Arrange 12 Js (large leaves) around Ks; appliqué. Appliqué 40 Ls (grapes) as shown.

**11.** Referring to photograph for placement, appliqué remaining Js and Ms to purple squares as shown.

**Quilting**

Quilt around appliquéd pieces. Quilt remainder in 2" crosshatch pattern.

**Finished Edges**

Bind with bias binding made from dark purple.

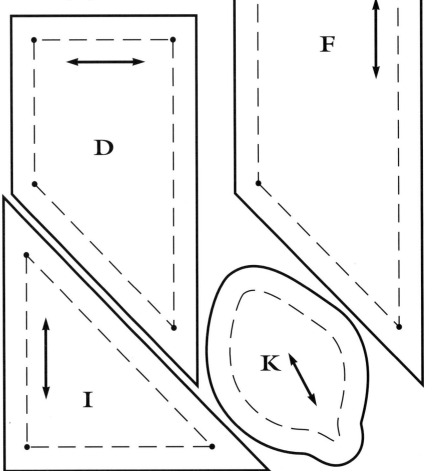

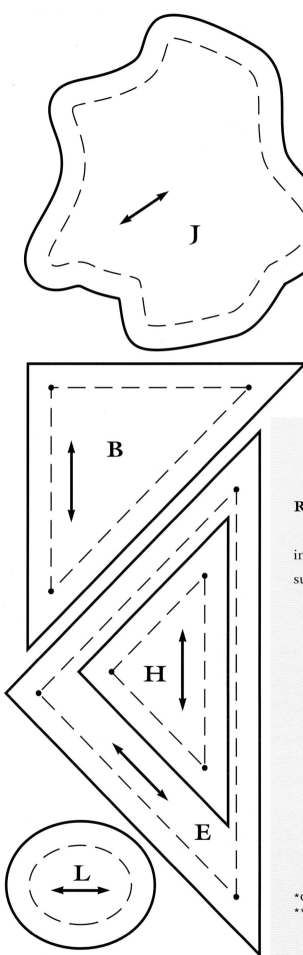

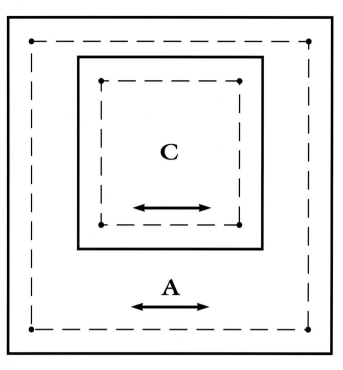

## ❖ QUILT SMART ❖

**Rotary-Cutting Instructions**

If you prefer rotary-cutting geometric pieces instead of tracing around templates, use these measurements to speed you on your way:

**A**– 3½" square. Cut 4 from floral.

**B**– 3" square*. Cut 8 squares from lavender, 16 from purple print 1, 8 from purple print 2.

**C**– 2" square. Cut 16 from floral.

**E**– 3⅞" square.* Cut 8 squares from pink/purple print and 8 from dark purple.

**G**– 2½" square. Cut 18 from purple print 1, 12 from magenta, and 960 from assorted prints.

**H**– 3¼" square.** Cut 36 squares from purple print 1, 24 from magenta, and 28 from assorted prints.

**I**– 2⅞" square.* Cut 46 squares from assorted prints.

*Cut each square in half diagonally to make 2 triangles.
**Cut each square into quarters diagonally to make 4 triangles.

# Granville Quilt and Needlework Guild
## Granville, Connecticut

$\mathcal{B}$orn during the national Bicentennial celebration in 1976, the Granville Quilt and Needlework Guild has emphasized community outreach from its beginning. Their first group project was a quilt raffled to raise money for the town of Granville, and charitable work has formed a solid core of their time together ever since.

"We make gift quilts for children who are patients at the Shriner Hospital in Springfield, Massachusetts," says Downy Koch, the guild's secretary. "It's a wonderful way for our newer members to improve their quilting skills while offering something worthwhile to the community." The gift quilts are often more than simple comforters; Downy describes an oversized quilted checkerboard with washable felt checkers as an example of one that entertains as well as soothes its recipient.

Members of the guild take every opportunity to promote the art of quilting. "We always have a hands-on exhibit at the regional Craft Adventure show held each August in Springfield," Downy says. "And several of our members, in elaborate 1860s-era costumes, demonstrate hand piecing and quilting each Christmas at a nearby historical village."

# Granville Star
## 1995

The Granville Star pattern was designed in 1976 by one of the members of the Granville Quilt and Needlework Guild for that first fund-raising quilt. "We wanted something that would appeal to quilters of varying skill levels," Downy Koch says. "We needed a pattern that would look good when made in scrap style or in a more controlled color scheme, and the Granville Star does all of that."

Although the pattern chosen for the annual raffle quilt varies each year, the guild members keep coming back to the Granville Star.

"We make another one every five years or so," Downy says. "Because it was designed by one of our members and named after our town, this quilt pattern is special to us."

Dark prints

    128 (3⅞") squares**

Brown

    2 (2" x 111½") borders

    2 (2" x 87½") borders

Blue

    2 (3½" x 117½") borders

    2 (3½" x 93½") borders

**Cut each in half for 2 triangles.

## Quilt Top Assembly

**1.** Referring to *Star Block Assembly Diagram*, join 16 light print triangles, 8 medium print triangles, and 8 dark print triangles as shown to make 1 star block. Repeat to make 32.

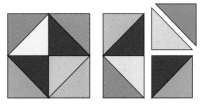

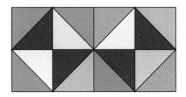

*Star Block Assembly Diagram*

**2.** To make 1 Snowball block, place 1 white square right side up on work surface. Aligning raw edges, pin 1 (3½") medium print square right side down on each corner, as shown in *Snowball Block Assembly Diagram, Figure 1.* Mark diagonal line across each square; stitch along lines. Trim corners ¼" from stitching, as shown in *Figure 2.* Discard triangles, or reserve for another project. Repeat to make 31 Snowball blocks.

## Granville Star

### Finished Quilt Size

93" x 117"

### Number of Blocks and Finished Size

| | |
|---|---|
| 32 Star Blocks | 12" x 12" |
| 31 Snowball Blocks | 12" x 12" |

### Fabric Requirements

| | |
|---|---|
| White | 4¼ yards |
| Light prints | 2 yards |
| Medium prints | 2 yards |
| Dark prints | 7½ yards |
| Brown | 3¼ yards |
| Blue | 3½ yards* |
| Backing | 8¼ yards |

*Includes fabric for bias binding.

### Pieces to Cut

White

    31 (12½") squares

Light prints

    256 (3⅞") squares**

Medium prints

    128 (3⅞") squares**

    124 (3½") squares

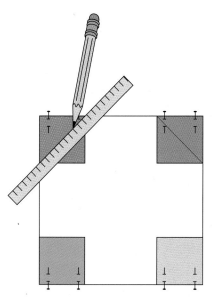

*Figure 1*

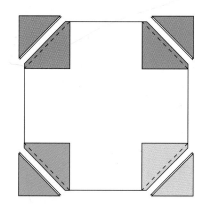

*Figure 2*

*Snowball Block Assembly Diagram*

**3.** To make odd-numbered rows, join 4 Star blocks alternately with 3 Snowball blocks as shown in *Quilt Top Assembly Diagram*. Repeat to make 5 odd-numbered rows. To make even-numbered rows, join 4 Snowball blocks alternately with 3 Star blocks as shown. Repeat to make 4 even-numbered rows. Join rows as shown.

**4.** Join 2" x 87½" brown borders to top and bottom of quilt. Join 2" x 111½" brown borders to sides of quilt, mitering corners.

**5.** Join 3½" x 93½" blue borders to top and bottom of quilt. Join 3½" x 117½" blue borders to sides of quilt, mitering corners.

## Quilting

Quilt diagonal lines across all star blocks as shown in photograph. Quilt Snowball blocks as desired.

## Finished Edges

Bind with bias binding made from blue.

*Quilt Top Assembly Diagram*

# Genessee Valley Quilt Club
## Rochester, New York

*Front row, l to r:* Jean Wentworth, Jeri Walmer McKay, Doris Leifer, Linda Kronenwetter, Carol P. Brickman, Leslie Ann Phillips, Kay Salerno, Lois Mae E. Kuh, Roslyn Smith, Shirley Few, Rosemary Brindisi Scholl, Anne Burton.

*Row 2, l to r:* Dolores Fanton, Sally Sexton, Donna Boddery, Sue Belik, Julie Havens Rittmeyer, Joanne Frazier, Ruth Norton, Mary Shaw, Joan Wigg, Karen Parrett, Shannon Banks, Carolyn B. Maruggi, Phyllis Sprague, Alice J. Sadue-Sakolow, Jean Grimm, Patty Rund.

*Row 3, l to r:* Evelyn Pengelly, Caroline Aman, Lenore B. Harvey, Marion Steger, Evelyn Marriott, Mildred Daley, Miriam Hoffman, Zylpha Suidara, Doris Fleming, Monica Marcotte, Irene Daniels, Pat Brice, Doris Coolidge, Hannelore Drewell, Sally Steiger, Edith Olson, Ruby Boergesson, Margaret Ames.

*Row 4, l to r:* Mary Mangan, Brenda Love, Connie Gomez, Patricia Faulkner, Clara Mogavero, Nancy LeVant, Dorothy Gerhard, Louise Hartshorn, M.L. "Hutch" Frederick, Carol Schulze, Marsha Lee, Ginny Schelkun, Judy Laurini, Nancy H. Gaede, Faith Kulp, Rosemary Bayer, Virginia McGuinness, Jan Herfindal, Dora Ryan, Maggie Weiss.

*Back row, l to r:* Sheila Thomas, Charlene Smith, Sue Vidro, Mel Ebert, Margaret Fahey, Beverly Wilson, Merilu O'Dell, Emily Ann O'Dell, Debby Taylor, Cindy Wallace, Debra Roach, Jodee Todd, Sandy Gray, Joan Wright, Deb Radzinski, Ann Russo, Pat Morrissey, Anne Gorman, Elaine Bolthouse, Linda Michael, Elizabeth Coombs, Lucille Harrigan, Ena Wait, Clare Wolcott.

# Springtime Jubilee
## 1995

Each year, the members of the Genessee Valley Quilt Club make a raffle quilt to raise money for their community works. "We usually hold the raffle at the springtime show," says Leslie Ann Phillips, one of the quilt's designers, "so we wanted a quilt that looked fresh and clean and spring-like." To involve as many members as possible, the design committee balanced intricate appliqué with a number of pieced blocks. To ensure consistent stitches and to create crisp clean curves, Leslie and co-designer Zylpha Suidara divided the appliqué volunteers into classes and taught them a method using spray starch and posterboard templates.

After Carolyn Maruggi assembled the quilt top, members at a monthly meeting helped baste it, and Peg Tuttle coordinated the efforts of 14 members to complete the quilting.

Springtime Jubilee *was designed by Leslie Ann Phillips, Carolyn Maruggi, and Zylpha Suidara. Appliqué, piecing, and quilting were completed by Peg Tuttle (chairman), Edith Clow, Karen Parrett, Marion Katerle, Joan Aceto, Monica Marcotte, Marilu O'Dell, Sue Belik, Elaine Bolthouse, Barbara Stoner, Jer McKay, Janice Baroody, Hutch Frederick, Evelyn Marriott, Ruth Norton, Peg Ames, Marlene White, Irene Daniels, Brenda Love, and Barbara Pudiak.*

## Springtime Jubilee

### Finished Quilt Size
90" x 102"

### Fabric Requirements

| | |
|---|---|
| White | 7 yards |
| Light green | ½ yard |
| Medium green | 2½ yards* |
| Dark green | ½ yard |
| Light purple | ¼ yard |
| Medium purple | ¼ yard |
| Dark purple | ¼ yard |
| Light yellow | ¼ yard |
| Medium yellow | ¼ yard |
| Dark yellow | ¼ yard |
| Light peach | ¼ yard |
| Medium peach | ¼ yard |
| Dark peach | ¼ yard |
| Light red | ¼ yard |
| Medium red | ¼ yard |
| Dark red | ¼ yard |
| Light magenta | ¼ yard |
| Medium magenta | ¼ yard |
| Dark magenta | ¼ yard |
| Floral | 2½ yards |
| Backing | 8¼ yards |

*Includes fabric for bias binding.

### Pieces to Cut

**White**
2 (13½" x 90¾") borders
4 (13½" x 38⅝") borders
1 (24½") square
2 (24⅜") squares**
608 (1½" x 3½") strips
29 (3½") squares†

**Light green**
8 D
4 D rev.
4 K
4 L
8 O
4 O rev.
2 DD
2 DD rev.
20 LL

**Medium green**
1 (20") square for bias
4 (1¼" x 26¾") strips
8 (1½" x 26¾") strips
8 (1½" x 33¼") strips
2 (1½" x 63¼") strips
28 (3½") squares††

**Dark green**
4 D rev.
4 E
4 K
4 K rev.
4 L
4 L rev.
4 Z
4 Z rev.
6 DD
10 DD rev.
20 LL

**Light purple**
1 C
2 EE
4 LL

**Medium purple**
1 B
4 F
2 FF
4 LL

**Dark purple**
1 A
4 G
2 GG
4 LL

**Light yellow**
1 C
8 J rev.
4 JJ
4 NN rev.

**Medium yellow**
1 B

8 I rev.
4 HH
4 NN

**Dark yellow**
1 A
4 H
4 T
2 U
4 CC
4 II

**Light peach**
1 C
4 D
4 J
4 CC

**Medium peach**
1 B
4 F
4 I
4 D rev.
4 BB

**Dark peach**
1 A
4 G
4 T
4 AA
4 MM

**Light red**
4 G

**Medium red**
8 F

**Dark red**
4 G

**Light magenta**
1 C
4 J
4 S
4 S rev.
4 Y
4 LL

**Medium magenta**
1 B
2 M
2 M rev.
4 I
4 R
4 R rev.
2 U
4 Y
4 LL

**Dark magenta**
1 A
2 M
2 M rev.
4 H
8 S
8 X
4 KK

**Floral**
304 (1½" x 3½") strips
4 N
4 V
4 P
4 W

120

**\*\*Cut each in half diagonally for 4 appliqué triangles.**

**†Cut each into quarters diagonally for 116 white border triangles.**

**††Cut each into quarters diagonally for 110 green border triangles. (You will have 2 triangles left over.)**

## Quilt Top Assembly

**1.** From 20" medium green square, make 375" of ⅞"-wide continuous bias strip. Press under ¼" on each long edge. Cut strip into stems as follows: 12 (1½") lengths, 144 (4") lengths, 4 (6") lengths, 32 (8") lengths, 1 (10") length, 2 (12") lengths, and 1 (24") length. Set aside.

**2.** To make center medallion, fold 24½" white square into quarters diagonally; finger-press to form appliqué placement guidelines. Unfold.

Referring to *Center Medallion Appliqué Placement Diagram*, appliqué 12 (4"-long) curved bias stems to square as shown. Appliqué 4 (8"-long) straight bias stems over curved stems, covering raw edges.

Using *Center Bias Guide*, lightly mark position of central curved octagon on center of square. Appliqué 10"-long bias strip to make octagon.

Referring to photograph for color placement and to *Center Medallion Appliqué Placement Diagram,* appliqué leaves (4 D, 4 D rev., 4 K, 4 L, 4 L rev., and 4 O) to square as shown. Appliqué flower pieces in this order: 4 A, 4 B, 4 C, 4 F, 4 G, 8 H, 4 I, 4 I rev., 4 J, 4 J rev., 4 M, 4 M rev., and 4 N.

Join 1 (1¼" x 26¾") medium green strip to each side of square, mitering corners, to complete medallion.

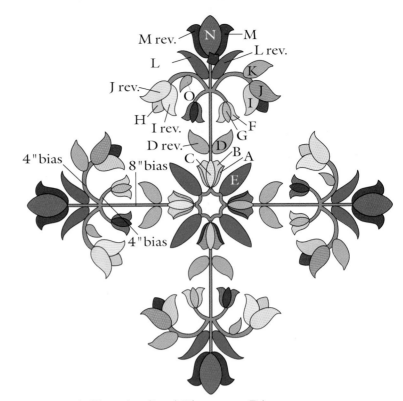

*Center Medallion Appliqué Placement Diagram*

*Quilt Top Assembly Diagram*

**3.** Join 2 (1½" x 3½") white strips to each side of 1 floral strip to make 1 pieced square. Repeat to make 21 pieced squares. Join squares into 6 rows, alternating direction in Rail Fence fashion, as shown in *Pieced Triangle Assembly Diagram.* Trim each end square to form triangle as shown in *Trimming Diagram.* Join rows to make 1 pieced triangle. Repeat to make 4 pieced triangles. Join pieced triangles to sides of center medallion.

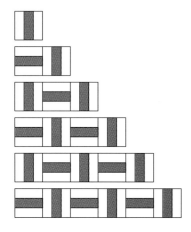

*Pieced Triangle Assembly Diagram*

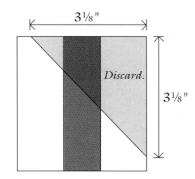

*Trimming Diagram*

**4.** Referring to photograph for color placement and to *Triangle Appliqué Placement Diagram,* appliqué 5 (4"-long) curved bias stems to 1 white triangle as shown. Appliqué 1 (4"-long) straight bias stem as shown, covering ends of curved

stems. Appliqué leaves (1 D, 1 D rev., 1 K, 1 K rev., 1 L, 1 L rev., 1 O, and 1 O rev.) as shown. Appliqué flower pieces in this order: 2 F, 2 G, 2 S, 1 Q, 1 Q rev., 1 R, 1 R rev., 2 T, 1 I, 1 I rev., 1 J, 1 J rev., 1 U, and 1 V.

Join 1 (1½" x 26¾") medium green strip to each short side of white triangle, mitering the corner, to complete 1 appliquéd triangle. Repeat to make 4 appliquéd triangles.

Join appliquéd triangles to sides of quilt as shown in *Quilt Top Assembly Diagram.*

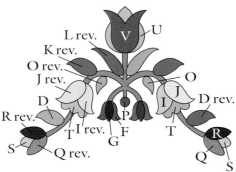

*Triangle Appliqué Placement Diagram*

**5.** To make 1 large pieced triangle, make 55 pieced squares as described in Step 3. Join squares, Rail Fence fashion, into 10 rows. Trim each end square to form triangle. Join rows.

Repeat to make 4 large pieced triangles.

**6.** To make 1 top pieced border, join 27 medium green triangles and 28 white triangles as shown in *Quilt Top Assembly Diagram.* Join 1 (1½" x 63¼") medium green strip to green edge of pieced strip.

Repeat to make bottom border.

**7.** In same fashion, join 14 medium green triangles and 15 white triangles to make 1 side

pieced border. Join 1 (1½" x 33¼") medium green strip to green edge of border. Repeat to make 4.

**8.** Join large pieced triangles to edges of quilt, as shown in *Quilt Top Assembly Diagram.* Join side pieced borders, with green strip innermost, to sides of triangles as shown. Join top and bottom borders, with green strip innermost, to top and bottom of quilt, mitering corners.

**9.** To make 1 appliquéd side border, fold 1 (13½" x 38⅝") white border in half vertically and horizontally to find center; finger-press to form appliqué placement guidelines. Unfold.

Referring to *Side Border Appliqué Placement Diagram,* appliqué 3 (1½"-long) bias flower stems to border as shown. Appliqué 1 (24"-long) bias stem to center of border. Referring to photograph for color placement, appliqué leaves (1 DD, 1 DD rev., 3 light green LLs, and 5 dark green LLs) as shown. Appliqué flower pieces in this order: 1 dark purple LL, 1 light purple LL, 1 medium purple LL, 1 KK, 1 medium magenta LL, 1 light magenta LL, 1 MM, 1 D rev., 1 D, 1 NN, 1 NN rev., and 1 CC.

Repeat to make 4 side borders.

**10.** Join borders to sides of quilt as shown in *Quilt Top Assembly Diagram.*

**11.** To make appliquéd top border, fold 1 (13½" x 90¾") white border in half vertically and horizontally to find center; finger-press to form appliqué placement guidelines. Unfold.

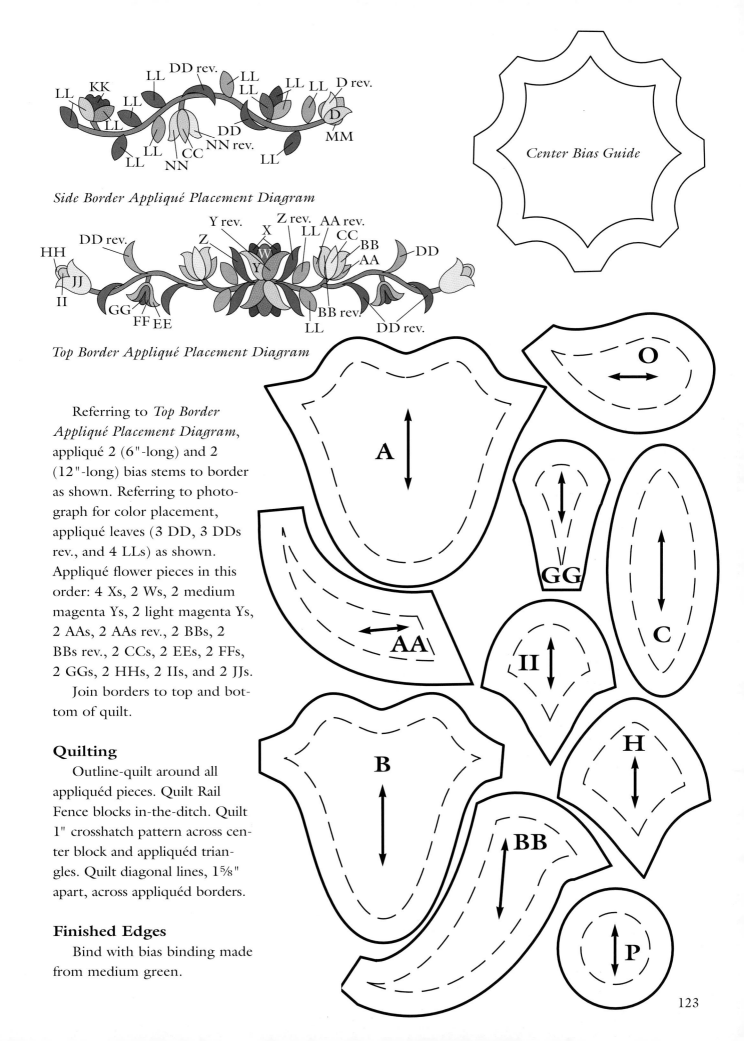

*Side Border Appliqué Placement Diagram*

*Top Border Appliqué Placement Diagram*

*Center Bias Guide*

Referring to *Top Border Appliqué Placement Diagram*, appliqué 2 (6"-long) and 2 (12"-long) bias stems to border as shown. Referring to photograph for color placement, appliqué leaves (3 DD, 3 DDs rev., and 4 LLs) as shown. Appliqué flower pieces in this order: 4 Xs, 2 Ws, 2 medium magenta Ys, 2 light magenta Ys, 2 AAs, 2 AAs rev., 2 BBs, 2 BBs rev., 2 CCs, 2 EEs, 2 FFs, 2 GGs, 2 HHs, 2 IIs, and 2 JJs.

Join borders to top and bottom of quilt.

## Quilting

Outline-quilt around all appliquéd pieces. Quilt Rail Fence blocks in-the-ditch. Quilt 1" crosshatch pattern across center block and appliquéd triangles. Quilt diagonal lines, 1⅝" apart, across appliquéd borders.

## Finished Edges

Bind with bias binding made from medium green.

123

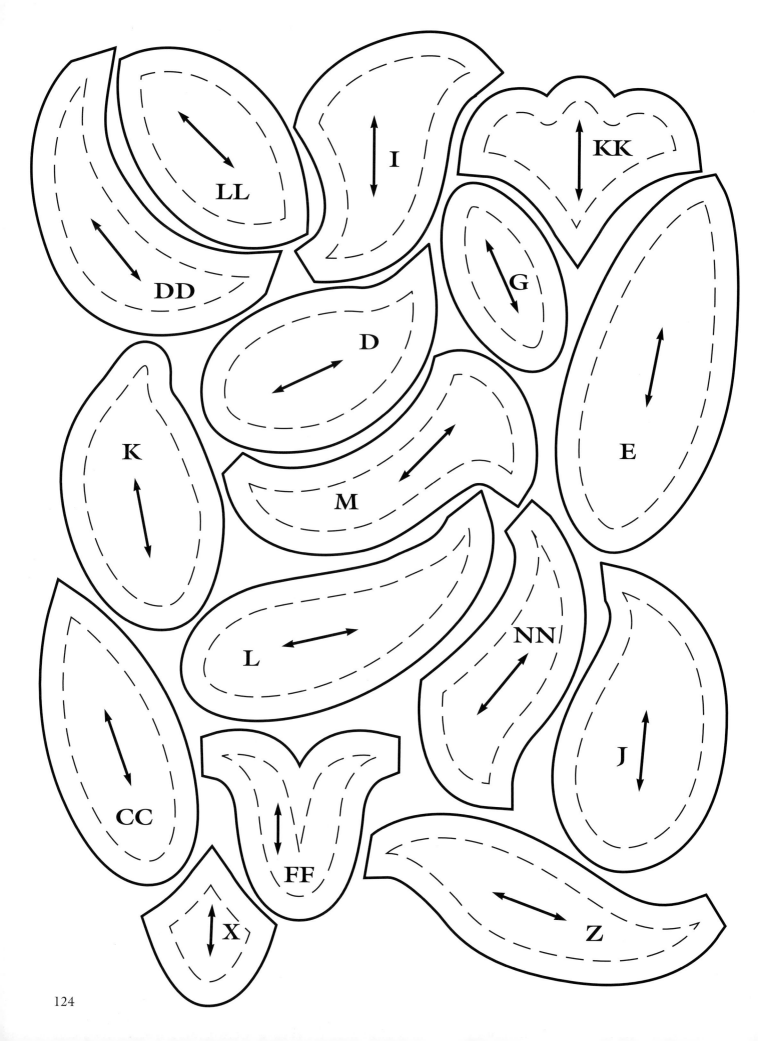

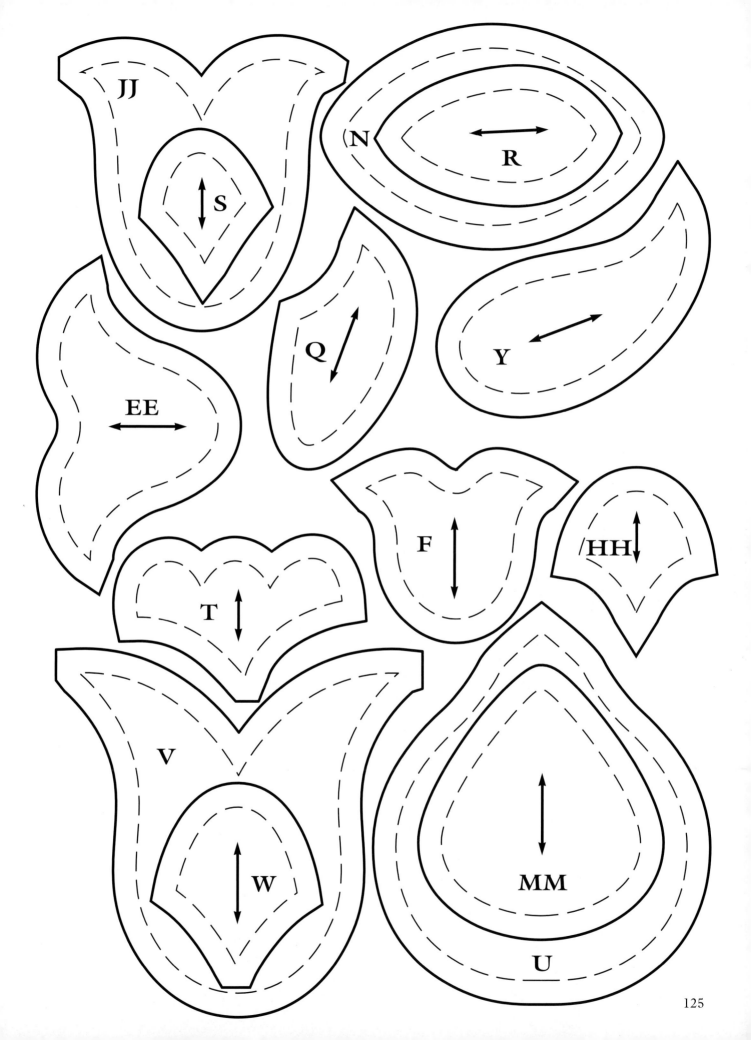

## Janine Hunt and Friends
### Bainbridge Island, Washington

*Front row, l to r: Peggy Schauer, Monique Noonan, Satrir Kaur, Georgie Carroll, Fabienne Assouad, Janine Hunt, Peggy Svendsen, Morag Aitken, Toshie Iijima.*
*Standing, l to r: Wong May Yin, Kazuko Kono, Margarita Nyler.*
*Not pictured: June Cheng, Ann Conn, Sue Dickie, Amy Ee, Teri Fung, Lynne Haley, Suzan Jensen, Dianne Kastern, Tutu Lane, Sue McMeans, June Morris, Muneko Nomatsu, Peggy Schaerer, Sawako Tsuneko, Chiemi Uemura.*

No matter where Janine Hunt has lived, she has found others who share her passion for quilting. "During the last eight or nine years of the two decades I lived in Singapore," she says, "a number of us from different countries formed a once-a-week quilting group. Every Tuesday morning we would meet in each others' homes to eat, talk, and sew."

The friends made baby quilts for new mothers among the group, farewell quilts for those moving away, and blocks to exchange at Christmas and birthdays. Many of the women first learned their quilting skills in the group, skills they would carry with them all over the world.

## Prairie Queen
### 1992

The blocks for *Prairie Queen* were Janine's going-away gift from her Tuesday quilting friends when she moved from Singapore to the Philippine Islands in 1992. Since the makers did not sign the blocks, Janine embroidered the name of each woman in the center of the block she had made.

"Fabienne Assouad, who now lives in Paris, set the blocks together with the scrappy star sashing," Janine says. "I quilted and finished the top to make a special remembrance of my friends so far away."

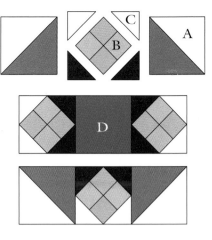

*Block Assembly Diagram*

## Prairie Queen

### Finished Quilt Size
80" x 88"

### Number of Blocks and Finished Size
30 blocks       9" x 9"

### Fabric Requirements
| | |
|---|---|
| White | 5¾ yards |
| Dark blue prints | 2½ yards |
| Red prints | ¾ yard |
| Light blue prints | ¾ yard |
| Pink prints | ¾ yard |
| Blue floral | 2¾ yards* |
| Backing | 5½ yards |

*Includes fabric for bias binding.

### Pieces to Cut
White
    2 (5" x 97½") borders
    2 (5" x 85½") borders
    93 (3½" x 9½") strips
    30 (3½") squares

    60 (3⅞") squares for A**
    120 (2⅜") squares for C**
Dark blue prints
    60 (3⅞") squares for A**
    72 (3½"-square) D
    336 (2") squares
Red prints
    120 (2⅜") squares for C**
Light blue prints
    240 (1⁹⁄₁₆"-square) B
Pink prints
    240 (1⁹⁄₁₆"-square) B
Blue floral
    2 (4" x 88½") borders
    2 (4" x 76½") borders
**Cut each in half for 2 triangles.

### Quilt Top Assembly
**1.** Referring to *Block Assembly Diagram*, join 4 white As, 4 dark blue print As, 8 light blue print Bs, 8 pink print As, 8 white Cs, 8 red print Cs, and 1 dark blue print D as shown to make 1 block. Repeat to make 30 blocks.

**2.** To make 1 sashing strip, place 1 (3½" x 9½") white strip right side up on work surface. Aligning raw edges, pin 1 (2") dark blue print square right side down on each corner, as shown in *Sashing Assembly Diagram, Figure 1*. Mark diagonal line across each square; stitch along lines. Trim corners ¼" from stitching, as shown in *Figure 2*. Discard triangles or reserve for another project. Repeat to make 71 sashing strips.

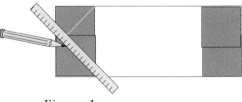

*Figure 1*

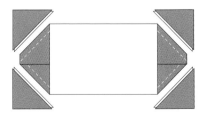

*Figure 2*

*Sashing Assembly Diagram*

**3.** To make 1 pieced sashing square, place 1 (3½") white square right side up on work surface. Aligning raw edges, pin 1 (2") dark blue print square right side down on 2 adjacent corners, as shown in *Sashing Square Assembly Diagram*. Mark, stitch, and trim corners as for sashing strip. Repeat to make 26 pieced sashing squares.

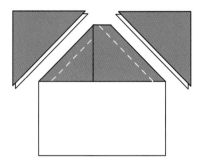

*Sashing Square Assembly Diagram*

**4.** To make top border row, join 6 pieced sashing squares alternately with 5 (3½" x 9½") white strips, beginning and ending with sashing square. Join 1 (3½") white square to each end of row, as shown in *Quilt Top Assembly Diagram*. Repeat to make bottom border row.

**5.** To make 1 sashing row, join 6 (3½") red print squares alternately with 5 sashing strips, beginning and ending with red print square. Join 1 pieced sashing square to each end of row, as shown in *Quilt Top Assembly Diagram*. Repeat to make 7 sashing rows.

**6.** To make 1 block row, join 6 sashing strips alternately with 5 blocks, beginning and ending with sashing strip. Join 1 (3½" x 9½") white strip to each end of row, as shown in

*Quilt Top Assembly Diagram*. Repeat to make 6 block rows.

**7.** Join sashing rows alternately with block rows, beginning and ending with sashing row. Join top and bottom pieced borders to top and bottom of quilt.

**8.** Join 4" x 76½" blue floral borders to top and bottom of quilt. Join 4" x 88½" blue floral borders to sides of quilt, mitering corners.

**9.** Join 5" x 85½" white borders to top and bottom of quilt. Join 5" x 97½" white borders to sides of quilt, mitering corners.

## Quilting

Outline-quilt around all pieces. Quilt feathers in sashing strips and borders, or quilt as desired.

## Finished Edges

Bind with bias binding made from blue floral.

*Quilt Top Assembly Diagram*

# Designer Gallery

## Jan Brashears
### Atlanta, Georgia

*M*issouri native Jan Brashears had lived in the South all her life when her husband's job took them to Michigan in the early 1980s. "I took quilting classes just to survive the winters that we weren't used to," she says. "On the first day of spring, 17" of snow fell. My husband's job there was a three-year assignment, but he was so eager to go back South he finished it in 10 months!"

*"Each step in making a quilt is fun. Each piece gains momentum as it evolves."*

Even though Jan is an accomplished and award-winning quilter, she firmly believes in the value of continuing her quilting education. "I encourage every quilter to take classes," she says. "Learning from a variety of teachers adds to your skills." It's also important for her to share ideas, techniques, and fabrics with other quilters. "Many traditional quilters don't realize that we who make contemporary quilts use the same techniques. Our fabrics and methods may be different, but our admiration for traditional work is always strong."

Any other advice? "Get cats!" she says. "Cats love everything about quilting, especially embellishments."

## Birds of a Feather #3: Crested Crane
### 1995

"I love working with birds because their feathers lend themselves so well to the kind of machine embellishment I like," Jan says. *Crested Crane* is the third in the *Birds of a Feather* series Jan began several years ago when a greeting card showing a parrot caught her eye. After completing two parrots, she was thinking about a third when *Zoom,* the magazine of Zoo Atlanta, published a photograph of a crested crane on its cover. "They're really very gray birds," Jan says. "I had pulled out all of my gray fabrics, but I wasn't pleased with what I had. Then a friend told me to use some of my wild batiks. The bird needed color!"

Jan's slightly wacky sense of humor extends to the private name she uses for the quilt. *"Birds of a Feather #3: Crested Crane* is too much of a mouthful!" she says. "So since he's a crane, we just call him Bob."

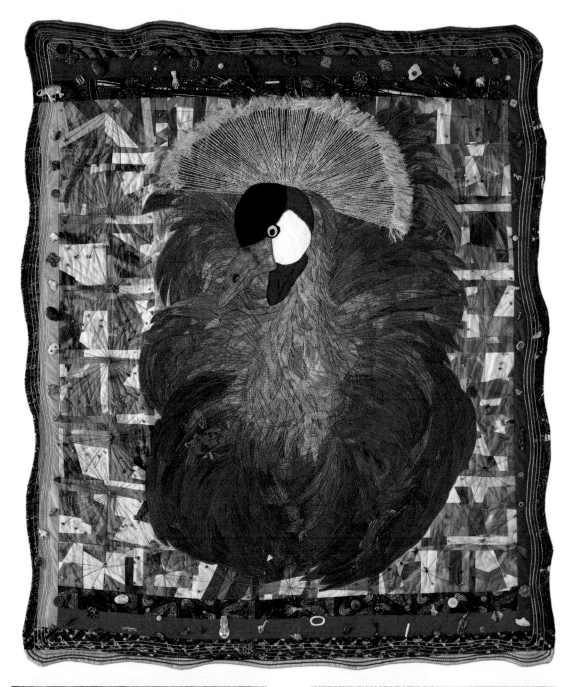

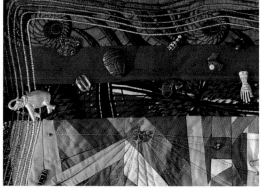

Jan loves to add "doodads" to her completed quilts. "Wherever I go, I look for unusual buttons and charms," she says. "Then I just add what I like to the quilt. It's done completely by instinct; no planning whatever."

To make the feather plumes, Jan twisted together several iridescent and metallic threads and then zigzag-stitched over them. After securing the loose ends, she frayed the last inch or so of each multiple strand.

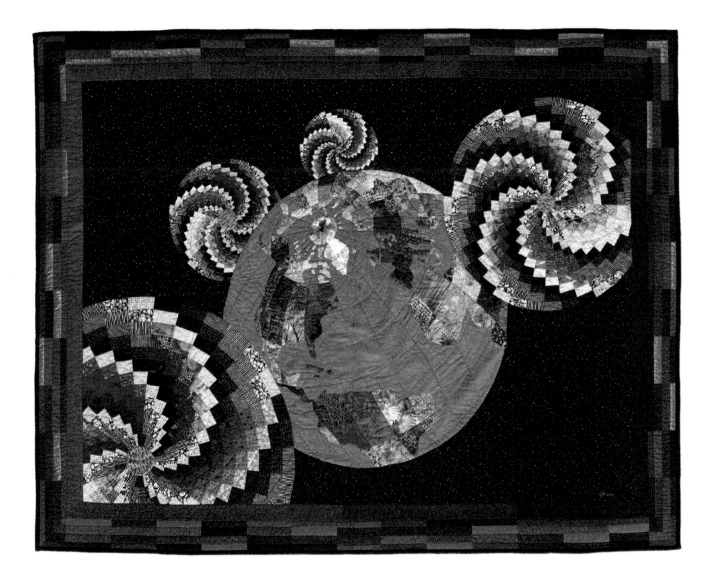

# Carolyn Craven
## Eagle, Idaho

$\mathcal{A}$t an early age, Carolyn Cravens learned to value needlework and other handmade items passed down through her family. "Afghans, cut-work linens, and quilts made by my grandmothers held special places in our house," Carolyn says. "My mom made her clothing and mine. Her sewing machine was set up in my room, so I feel a tremendous connection to these women."

*"Each and every quilter, past and present, is an artist."*

By the time of the U.S. Bicentennial, Carolyn was intrigued enough to take a beginning quilt class at the YMCA. For a number of years she made traditional quilts; but after she began taking art classes, she started designing her own.

"I love working in fiber because it honors the women from the past who worked so hard to make their families comfortable," Carolyn says. "It feels good to carry on their warmth and compassion in the art of quiltmaking."

## Somewhere Under the Rainbows
### 1994

Several years ago, artist and mom Carolyn Craven was asked to teach a lesson on color to her son's first-grade class. "We were going to paint color wheels," Carolyn says. "And I wanted them to really look at a rainbow before painting." She turned out all the lights in the classroom and shone one strong beam of light through a prism. "When the rainbows danced all around the room, the children oohed and aahed in wonder."

Carolyn used that prismatic rainbow in developing the spinning color wheels in her quilt. "Everything gets translated back to fabric!" she says. She drafted the globe with its lines of latitude and longitude, and carefully chose fabrics to represent the continents and the Arctic ice cap. "The variegated blue border fabrics depict the differing values of the daytime sky," she says, "and the quilting lines represent the contour lines of space."

# Linda S. Schmidt
## Dublin, California

"My idea of a good quilt," says Linda Schmidt, "is one that takes my whole self and challenges me to make the idea real so that others can see it."

Although her pictorial quilts are showstoppers wherever they appear, Linda claims she can't draw. "My quilts usually exist somewhat blurrily in my head for quite some time before they become real." She explains that she cuts and sews and rips and re-sews each piece repeatedly until she has completed what she originally envisioned. "And I still don't like it until I've changed it some more, put on a border, added stitchery or embroidery or beads," she says. "And then it's okay, it's done, and people wonder at all the time it must have taken to put that piece together. They don't realize that I can't *not* do it. It would drive me crazy not to do it."

A bit impatient with admirers who call her an artist, Linda responds, "All quilters are artists! Quilts are a little bit of our souls. They are our heritage; they are our gift to the future."

*"The world cries out for color and beauty, comfort and caring, and that's what quiltmakers are all about."*

# The Dawn of Time
## 1996

In the fall of 1995, Linda became interested in a competition with the theme "Artistic Expressions" that called for new quilts made using styles, colors, or themes reminiscent of a famous artist.

Linda began by combining ideas from two 19th-century English painters: a pencil sketch of Stonehenge done by John Constable, and the color palette favored by J.M.W. Turner. "I had been to Stonehenge and been struck by both its massive beauty and the mystery behind its construction," Linda says. "In his paintings, Turner emphasized the forces of nature, often portraying clouds and wind as giant waves, with swirling skies and glowing colors." *The Dawn of Time*, the quilt's front side, portrays Stonehenge at dawn, with ominous clouds threatening the grand, mysterious structure. "But since no one really knows who built Stonehenge, or why," Linda adds, "I made the back to represent these unanswered questions and called it *Only the Shadow Knows*."

*The Dawn of Time*

*Only the Shadow Knows*

*Quilt design ©1994 by Corinne Appleton*

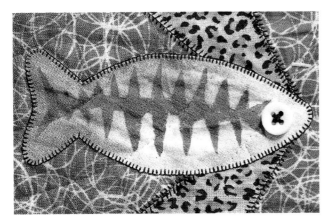

Corinne painted the skeletons on each of the fish in the border not once, but twice. "I first stenciled the skeletons, but my enthusiasm overrode my common sense, and I forgot to add textile medium to the paint," she says. "When the quilt was washed, most of the paint flaked off. Because the stencil no longer fit the quilt, I was stuck with the scary and tedious job of hand-painting the skeletons on the completed piece. Lesson learned!"

Using a roll of telephone wire, Corinne gave this kitty three-dimensional whiskers after the quilting was completed. "Using a blunt needle to force the threads apart, I coaxed a length of wire under the upper layer of fabric," she says. "Then I twisted each end around a thin dowel to create curls and kinks. The whiskers won't easily pull out but can be removed for cleaning, if necessary."

138

## Corinne Appleton
### Jacksonville, Florida

"*I* can't draw or sculpt or do any of the traditional art exercises," says Corinne Appleton. "My art teachers from school would be astonished at my emergence as a quiltmaker."

A longtime interest in interior design and decorating led Corinne to collect fabric for years without quite knowing how she would use it. In 1987, the birth of her first niece prompted her to make a baby quilt, but she didn't really start quilting until years later. After seeing her first quilt show, Corinne joined a local guild, bought a new sewing machine, and was ready to start sewing for the first time in several years. "Unfortunately, the machine was defective," she says dryly. "It took two more years of struggling before I realized it was the machine, not me!"

*"Know yourself and work to please yourself. The quilts you produce under those circumstances will be your best."*

Corinne credits her father's unwavering support for her success. "Dad was always there to tell me I had a special touch or a wonderful eye for color," she says. "He pushed and pulled me into finding my voice as a quiltmaker."

## A Tail of 12 Kitties
### 1994

"I often get comments from people that indicate they believe my quilts spring to life easily and magically," Corinne says. "*Puhleese!* There's often agony involved."

*A Tail of 12 Kitties,* like most of Corinne's work, celebrates the many cats who have shared her life and the many who are yet to come. Her playful sense of humor ("goofiness," she calls it) shows in the crossed eyes of one of the cats and the particularly stubborn character who turns his back to keep his portrait from being made. The border of leopardskin swags and fish "tassels," a tongue-in-cheek referral to the elaborate borders used on Baltimore Album quilts, is another example.

"The tassels had me stumped for a long while," Corinne says. "Then I thought of fish. It occurred to me that since my kitties are happy, they must be well-fed. So all that would be left would be the skeletons of the fish!"

# QUILT SMART WORKSHOP
## A Guide to Quiltmaking

❖

### Preparing Fabric

Before cutting out any pieces, be sure to wash and dry your fabric to preshrink it. All-cotton fabrics may need to be pressed before cutting. Trim selvages from the fabric before you cut your pieces.

### Making Templates

Before you can make one of the quilts in this book, you must make templates from the printed pattern pieces given. Quilters have used many materials to make templates, including cardboard and sandpaper. Transparent template plastic, available at craft supply and quilt shops, is durable, see-through, and easy to use.

To make templates using plastic, place the plastic sheet on the printed page and trace the pattern piece, using a laundry marker or permanent fine-tip marking pen. For machine piecing, trace along the outside solid (cutting) line. For hand piecing, trace along the inside broken (stitching) line. Cut out the template along the traced line. Label each template with the pattern name, letter, grain line arrow, and match points (corner dots).

### Marking and Cutting Fabric

Place the template facedown on the wrong side of the fabric and mark around the template with a sharp pencil. Move the template (see next two paragraphs) and continue marking pieces; mark several before you stop to cut.

If you will be piecing your quilt by machine, the pencil lines represent the cutting lines. Leave about ¼" between pieces as you mark. Cut along the marked lines.

For hand piecing, the pencil lines are the seam lines. Leave at least ¾" between marked lines for seam allowances. Add ¼" seam allowance around each piece as you cut. Mark match points (corner dots) on each piece.

### Hand Piecing

To hand piece, place two fabric pieces together with right sides facing. Insert a pin in each match point of the top piece. Stick the pin through both pieces and check to be sure that it pierces the match point on the bottom piece *(Figure 1)*. Adjust the pieces if necessary to align the match points. (The raw edges of the two pieces may not be exactly aligned.) Pin the pieces securely together.

Sew with a running stitch of 8 to 10 stitches per inch. Checking your stitching as you go to be sure that you are stitching in the seam line of both pieces, sew from match point to match point. To make sharp corners, begin and end the stitching exactly at the match point; do not stitch into the seam allowances. When joining units where several seams come together, do not sew over seam allowances; sew through them at the point where all seam lines meet *(Figure 2)*.

Always press both seam allowances to one side. Pressing the seam open, as in dressmaking, may leave gaps between the stitches through which quilt batting may beard. Press seam allowances toward the darker fabric whenever you can. When four or more seams meet at one point, such as at the corner of a block, press all the seams in a "swirl" in the same direction to reduce bulk *(Figure 3)*.

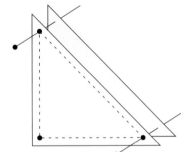

1—*Aligning Match Points*

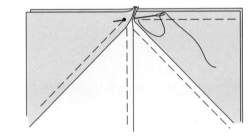

2—*Joining Units*

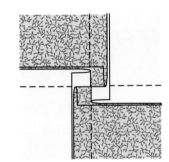

3—*Pressing Intersecting Seams*

### Machine Piecing

To machine piece, place two fabric pieces together with right sides facing. Align match points as described under "Hand Piecing" and pin the pieces together securely.

Set your stitch length at 12 to 15 stitches per inch. At this setting, you will not need to backstitch to lock seam beginnings and ends. Use a presser foot that gives a perfect

¼" seam allowance, or measure ¼" from the sewing machine needle and mark that point on the presser foot with nail polish or masking tape.

Chain-piece sections, stitching edge to edge, to save time when sewing similar sets of pieces *(Figure 4)*. Join the first two pieces as usual. At the end of the seam, do not backstitch, cut the thread, or lift the presser foot. Instead, sew a few stitches off the fabric. Place the next two pieces and continue stitching. Keep sewing until all the sets are joined. Then cut the sets apart.

Press seam allowances toward the darker fabric. When you join blocks or rows, press the seam allowances of the top piece in one direction and the seam allowances of the bottom piece in the opposite direction to help ensure that the seams will lie flat *(Figure 5)*.

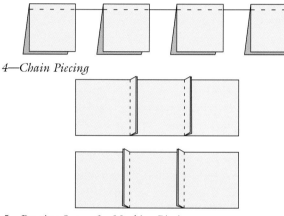

*4—Chain Piecing*

*5—Pressing Seams for Machine Piecing*

## Hand Appliqué

Hand appliqué is the best way to achieve the look of traditional appliqué. However, using freezer paper, which is sold in grocery stores, can save a lot of time because it eliminates the need for hand basting the seam allowances.

Make templates without seam allowances. Trace the template onto the *dull* side of the freezer-paper and cut the paper on the marked line. Make a freezer paper shape for each piece to be appliquéd. Pin the freezer-paper shape, with its *shiny side up,* to the *wrong side* of your fabric. Following the paper shape and adding a scant ¼" seam allowance, cut out the fabric piece. Do not remove the pins. Using the tip of a hot, dry iron, press the seam allowance to the shiny side of the freezer paper. Be careful not to touch the shiny side of the freezer paper with the iron. Remove the pins.

Pin the appliqué shape in place on the background fabric. Use one strand of sewing thread in a color to match the appliqué shape. Using a very small slipstitch *(Figure 6)* or blindstitch *(Figure 7)*, appliqué the shape to the background fabric.

After your stitching is complete, cut away the background fabric behind the appliqué shape, leaving ¼" seam allowance. Separate the freezer paper from the fabric with your fingernail and pull gently to remove it.

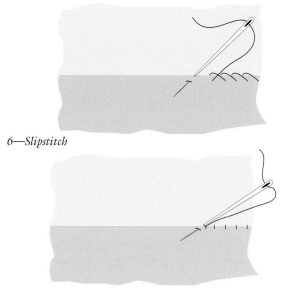

*6—Slipstitch*

*7—Blindstitch*

## Mitering Borders

Mitered borders take a little extra care to construct. First, measure your quilt. Cut two border strips to fit the shorter of two opposite sides, plus the width of the border plus 2". Now center the measurement for the shorter side on one border strip and place a pin at each end of the measurement. Match the pins on the border strip to the corners of the longer side of the quilt. Join the border strip to the quilt, easing the quilt to fit between the pins and stopping ¼" from each corner of the quilt *(Figure 8)*. Join the remaining cut strip to the opposite end of the quilt. Cut and join the remaining borders in the same manner. Press seams to one side. Follow *Figures 9 and 10* to miter corners.

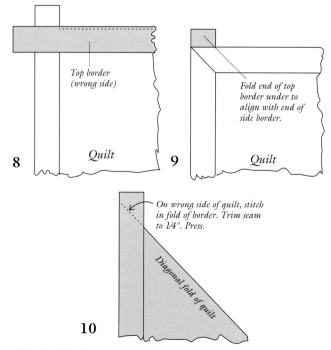

*Mitering Borders*

## Marking Your Quilt Top

After the quilt top is completed, it should be thoroughly pressed and then marked with quilting designs. The most popular methods for marking use stencils or templates. Both can be purchased, or you can make your own. Use a silver quilter's pencil for marking light to medium fabrics and a white artist's pencil on dark fabrics. Lightly mark the quilt top with your chosen quilting designs.

## Making a Backing

While some fabric and quilt shops sell 90" and 108" widths of backing fabric, the instructions in *Great American Quilts* give backing yardage based on 45"-wide fabric. When using 45"-wide fabric, all quilts wider than 42" will require a pieced backing. For quilts whose width measures between 42" and 80", purchase an amount of fabric equal to two times the desired length of the unfinished quilt backing. (The unfinished quilt backing should be at least 3" larger on all sides than the quilt top.)

The backing fabric should be of a type and color that is compatible with the quilt top. Percale sheets are not recommended because they are tightly woven and difficult to hand-quilt through.

A pieced backing for a bed quilt should have three panels. The three-panel backing is recommended because it tends to wear better and lie flatter than the two-panel type, the center seam of which often makes a ridge down the center of the quilt. Begin by cutting the fabric in half widthwise (*Figure 11*). Open the two lengths and stack them, with right sides facing and selvages aligned. Stitch along both selvage edges to create a tube of fabric (*Figure 12*). Cut down the center of the top layer of fabric *only* and open the fabric flat (*Figure 13*).

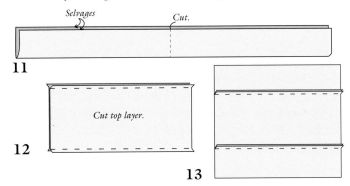

*Making a Three-Panel Backing*

## Layering and Basting

Prepare a working surface to spread out the quilt. Place the backing on the working surface right side down. Unfold the batting and place it on top of the backing. Smooth any wrinkles or lumps in the batting.

Lay the quilt top right side up on top of the batting and backing. Make sure the backing and quilt top are aligned. Knot a long strand of sewing thread and use a darning needle for basting. Begin basting in the center of your quilt and baste out toward the edges. The stitches should cover an ample amount of the quilt so that the quilt layers do not shift during quilting. Inadequate basting can result in puckers and folds on the back and front of the quilt.

## Hand Quilting

Hand quilting can be done with the quilt in a hoop or in a floor frame. It is best to start quilting in the middle of your quilt and work out toward the edges.

Most quilters use a very thin, short needle called a "between." Betweens are available in sizes 7 to 12, with 7 being the longest and 12 the shortest. If you are a beginning quilter, try a size 7 or 8. Because betweens are so much shorter than other hand-sewing needles, they may feel awkward at first. As your skill increases, try switching to a smaller needle to help you make smaller stitches.

Quilting thread, heavier and stronger than ordinary sewing thread, is available in a wide variety of colors. But if color matching is critical and you can't find the color you need, you may substitute cotton sewing thread. We suggest you coat it with beeswax before quilting to prevent it from tangling and knotting.

To begin, thread your needle with an 18" to 24" length and make a small knot at one end. Insert the needle into the top of the quilt approximately ½" from the point you want to begin quilting. Do not take the needle through all three layers, but stop it in the batting and bring it up through the quilt top again at your starting point. Tug gently on the thread to pop the knot through the quilt top into the batting. This anchors the thread without an unsightly knot showing on the back. With your non-sewing hand underneath the quilt, insert the needle with the point straight down in the quilt about ¹⁄₁₆" from the starting point. With your underneath finger, feel for the point as the needle comes through the backing (*Figure 14*). Place the thumb of your sewing hand approximately ½" ahead of your needle. At the moment you feel the needle touch your underneath finger, push the fabric up from below as you rock the needle down to a nearly horizontal position. Using the thumb of your sewing hand in conjunction with the underneath hand, pinch a little hill in the fabric and push the tip of the needle back through the quilt top (*Figure 15*).

Now either push the needle all the way through to complete one stitch or rock the needle again to an upright position on its point to take another stitch. Take no more than a quarter-needleful of stitches before pulling the needle through.

When you have about 6" of thread remaining, you must end the old thread securely and invisibly. Carefully tie a knot in the thread, flat against the surface of the fabric. Pop the knot through the top as you did when beginning the line of quilting. Clip the thread, rethread your needle, and continue quilting.

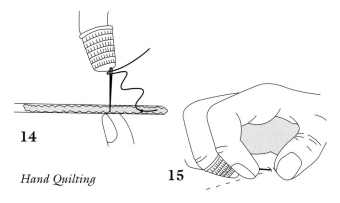

**14**

*Hand Quilting*    **15**

## Machine Quilting

Machine quilting is as old as the sewing machine itself; but until recently, it was thought inferior to hand quilting. Machine quilting does, however, require a different set of skills from hand quilting.

Machine quilting can be done on your sewing machine using a straight, even stitch and a special presser foot. A walking foot, or even-feed foot, is recommended for straight-line machine quilting to help the top fabric move through the machine at the same rate that the feed dogs move the bottom fabric. With free-motion machine quilting, use a darning foot to protect your fingers and to prevent skipped stitches.

Regular sewing thread or nylon thread can be used for machine quilting. With the quilt top facing you, roll the long edges of the basted quilt toward the center of the quilt, leaving a 12"-wide area unrolled in the center. Secure the roll with bicycle clips, metal bands that are available at quilt shops. Begin at one unrolled end and fold the quilt over and over until only a small area is showing. This will be the area where you will begin to machine quilt.

Place the folded portion of the quilt in your lap. Start machine quilting in the center and work to the right side of the quilt, unfolding and unrolling the quilt as you go. Remove the quilt from the machine, turn it, and reinsert it in the machine to stitch the left side. A table placed behind your sewing machine will help support the quilt as it is stitched.

Curves and circles are most easily made by free-motion machine quilting. Using a darning foot and with the feed dogs down, move the quilt under the needle with movements of your fingertips. Place your fingertips on the fabric on each side of the presser foot and run your machine at a steady, medium speed. The length of the stitches is determined by the rate of speed at which you move the fabric through the machine. Do not rotate the quilt; rather, move it from side to side as needed. Always stop with the needle down to keep the quilt from shifting.

## Making Binding

A continuous bias strip is frequently used by quilters for all kinds of quilts but is especially recommended for quilts with curved edges. Follow these steps to make a continuous bias strip:

**1.** To make continuous bias binding, you'll need a square of fabric. Multiply the number of inches of binding needed by the desired width of the binding (usually 2½"). Use a calculator to find the square root of that number. That's the size square needed to make your binding.

**2.** Cut the square in half diagonally.

**3.** With right sides facing, join triangles to form a sawtooth as shown in *Figure 16*.

**4.** Press seam open. Mark off parallel lines the desired width of the binding as shown in *Figure 17*.

**5.** With right sides facing, align raw edges marked Seam 2. As you align the edges, extend a Seam 2 point past its natural matching point by the distance of the width of the bias strip as shown in *Figure 18*. Join.

**6.** Cut the binding in a continuous strip, starting with the protruding point and following the marked lines around the tube.

**7.** Press the binding strip in half lengthwise, with wrong sides facing. This gives you double-fold, or French-fold, binding, which is sturdier than single-fold binding.

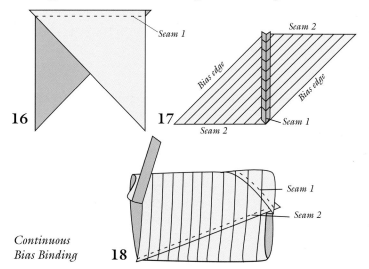

*Continuous Bias Binding*    **18**

## Attaching Binding

To prepare your quilt for binding, baste the layers together ¼" from the edge of the quilt. Trim the backing and batting even with the edge of the quilt top. Beginning at the midpoint of one side of the quilt, pin the binding to the top, with right sides facing and raw edges aligned.

Stitch the binding along one edge of the quilt, sewing through all layers. If you are machine-stitching, backstitch at the beginning of the seam to lock the stitching.

Stitch until you reach the seam line point at the corner, and backstitch. Lift the presser foot and turn the quilt to stitch along the next edge. Continue stitching around the edge. Join the beginning and ending of the binding strip by machine, or stitch one end by hand to overlap the other.

Turn the binding to the back side and blindstitch in place. At each corner, fold the excess binding neatly and blindstitch in place.

# RESOURCES

**Pages 9 and 36:** Both Helen White's *Night Sky* and Meg Simle's *Happy Fish* are based on block units from Doreen Speckmann's book *Pattern Play*, published by C&T Publishing, 5021 Blum Road #1, Martinez, CA 94553. Ask your local quilt shop to order a copy, or call (800) 284-1114 to order direct from the publisher.

**Page 14:** Joanna Lotts enlarged the cardinal block in the center of *Mama's Quilt* from a pattern in Margaret Rolfe's book *Go Wild With Quilts*, published by That Patchwork Place, P.O. Box 118, Bothell, WA 98041-0118. Call (800) 426-3126 for ordering information.

**Page 19:** For decorative rayon thread and invisible nylon thread like that Joanna Lotts used in quilting *Mama's Quilt*, contact the following suppliers:

Nancy's Notions, Ltd., 333 Beichl Ave., P.O. Box 683, Beaver Dam, WI 53916-0683; (800) 833-0690.

Clotilde, Inc., 2 Sew Smart Way Box B 8031, Stevens Point, WI 54481-8031; (800) 772-2891.

**Page 56:** Patterns for several house and tree quilts similar to Bette Haddon's *Cabin in the Woods* may be found in Janet Kime's book *Quilts to Share: Quick & Easy Quilts*, published by That Patchwork Place (address above).

**Page 110:** Gradated solids, such as the purples used for grapes in *Twilight*, may be ordered from the following suppliers:

Keepsake Quilting, P.O. Box 1618, Centre Harbor, NH 03226; (603) 253-8731. Item #5239, Shrinking Violet Medley.

Cherrywood Fabrics, Inc., P.O. Box 486, Brainerd, MN 56401; (218) 829-0967. Item #232, 8-Step Gradation, Eggplant to Light.

## Metric Conversion Chart

| | | | |
|---|---|---|---|
| ⅛ " | 3 mm | ⅛ yard | 0.11 m |
| ¼ " | 6 mm | ¼ yard | 0.23 m |
| ⅜ " | 9 mm | ⅜ yard | 0.34 m |
| ½ " | 1.3 cm | ½ yard | 0.46 m |
| ⅝ " | 1.6 cm | ⅝ yard | 0.57 m |
| ¾ " | 1.9 cm | ¾ yard | 0.69 m |
| ⅞ " | 2.2 cm | ⅞ yard | 0.80 m |
| 1 " | 2.5 cm | 1 yard | 0.91 m |

# Index to Quilt Smart Techniques

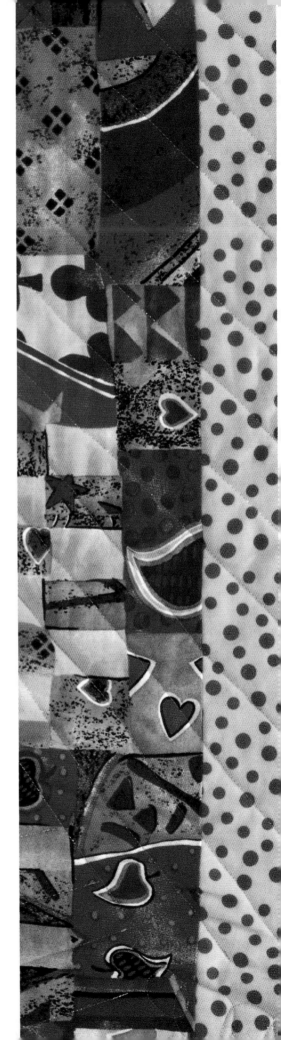